Joe's book took me back to a happy time when I could ride my bike downtown to the corner confectionery, enjoy a chocolate soda, and ride back home without a worry in the world! Heartwarming memories.

—Anne Ferguson Monahan, TCHS Class of 1965,
Miss Tuscola 1964

Joe Colwell's remembrances of Tuscola are my memories too. It has been exciting to read and discuss with my three sons these reflections of a wonderful community to grow up in.

—Bill Englehardt, TCHS Class of 1966,
Former Principal of East Prairie Elementary School, Tuscola

In preserving his memories of Tuscola, Joe Colwell has painted a literary Norman Rockwell of mid-century America. If you stitched together every iconic reference Hollywood has ever made to mid-century America, you would have to conclude that the cultural and geographical center of it was Tuscola, Illinois. The proof is in this book.

—David Porter, TCHS Class of 1983,
Editor and Publisher of *Tuscola Review* newspaper

When I finished reading Joe's book, all I could say was "wow." It brought back so many memories of a time when we were still naive and yet to experience the world ahead. I want to share with my children, maybe then they can get a better understanding of why I still call Tuscola home even though I now live in South Carolina.

—Donna Ard Braden, TCHS Class of 1965

The memory of my home town has lived in my mind and heart from the time I moved away over 52 years ago. I knew it was a special place to me when I lived there and I grieved for a long time over having to move away. How exciting it has been to look through Joe Colwell's eyes as he shares the tale of his life growing up in that small Midwestern town of Tuscola, Illinois, and to find that many of my own memories of such a special place and time are ones that someone else experienced. Somehow that fact makes my own memories more credible. Joe's work is a legacy for those living in this time but more importantly I find it a fitting memorial to those that helped shape and build the community of Tuscola during the years following World War II. It was their efforts that created the community we had the privilege of growing up in, and now through Joe's storytelling that unique time is revisited.

—Michelle Motta Lustig, former Tuscola resident.

A look into the past at growing up in Tuscola during the 1950s and '60s. It was a great and wonderful time during those early years of our childhood and on into teenage years. Brings back many memories that I hadn't thought of in years. Really captures life and times of life in Tuscola, Illinois, small town America.

—Howard E. Connour, TCHS Class of 1966

Joe Colwell's book is a personal reflection of coming of age in Tuscola. While my memories and interactions differ (regrettably no summer baseball for the girls) every page prompted memories of my own. The sites, the smells, the sounds as seasons passed in the middle of a century in the middle West are the ones we share. The pleasure and fun of his book goes beyond the dates of events to beginning to feel again the life and breath of childhood in that wonderful place.

—Maureen Deaver Purcell, TCHS Class of 1966,
Miss Tuscola 1966

TUSCOLA:
A MEMOIR

ALSO BY JOSEPH COLWELL

From Lichen Rock Press

Canyon Breezes: Exploring Magical Places in Nature
Zephyr of Time: Meditations on Time and Nature
Tales of Ravens Nest: A Life, A Place: Stories and Reflections
Echoes of Time: Reflections on the Mesas and Canyons of the
Dominguez-Escalante National Conservation Area

From Page Publishing

Sands of Time: A Flight of Discovery
and Search for Meanings of Time

TUSCOLA:
A MEMOIR

*Place, Time, and Meanings
of a Hometown*

JOSEPH COLWELL

Introduction by Michael G. Carroll

Lichen Rock Press
Hotchkiss, Colorado 81419

Editing: Katherine Colwell
Design and publishing services: Constance King Design

Lichen Rock Press
Hotchkiss, Colorado
ColwellCedars.com

ISBN: 978-0-9962222-4-2
Printed in USA

CONTENTS

PART III
MEANINGS

INTRODUCTION

A town, a railroad station, a train setting off with a young man, a starting place, a beginning. It recedes behind us and vanishing with all those green and gold summer mornings of boyhood, the air smelling like brown sugar, the cicadas' metronomic droning. A beginning...a starting place always there behind us, in memory. And the past decomposes into the bright dust of dreams...

Richard Lingeman, *Small Town America*

JOE COLWELL REMEMBERS the special time of life in middle America that Lingeman so lyrically paints: a bucolic image of life in small town America at its best, during a time when we played outdoors all summer day long—round robin baseball, war, hide-go-seek, exploring ditch banks with friends, laying pennies on railroad rails to be flattened by the iron monsters that rumbled by. Always safe from harm, always returning home to parents who loved us, when doors were left unlocked, and the world seemed to make sense.

Joe Colwell writes about the halcyon days of the 1950's and early 60's, before the Vietnam War intervened with its brutal reality, tearing America apart, shattering innocent dreams, scattering Joe and his classmates out into the world, the past decomposing "into the bright dust of dreams." His essays about Tuscola—his hometown—capture all its flavors and memories, reconstituting the "bright dust of dreams" back into reality, as if it were yesterday.

Born in May 1947, Joe was a first wave Baby Boomer. The second Great War had been won. Now was the time for peace, rebuilding, and the start of an industrial boom that would spread prosperity throughout the nation, even in Tuscola with its new industrial plant west of town. He literally grew up next to the town's three major rail lines that ran east and west: the C. & E. I, Missouri Pacific, and Baltimore and Ohio. Just three blocks west, the north and south line of the Illinois Central railroad connected Chicago to the Gulf of Mexico. These great national lines intersected just a few blocks from Joe's house. Tuscola was a railroad town and all of us who grew up here were forever affected by their presence.

Joe's home was 204 East North Central Avenue—one block from downtown—a one and a half story, simple wood frame house that faced south. It was a close family: Joe's father R.B. "Bob," his mother Ruby, and older brother Ron. And Wiggles the dog. My memory of visiting in the evening are almost always of R.B., leaning back in his easy chair, watching television, often yelling at liberal newscasters criticizing America. Ruby would walk out of the kitchen, where she had been cooking, through the dining room and into the front room, and smile at me. She always seemed to be smiling, this still beautiful woman, the first "Miss Tuscola" crowned back in the Depression. Ron was always around, but, being six years older than Joe and me, mostly ignored us.

Joe's essays perfectly capture the times of our youth. His memory is sharp, his imagery evocative, his writing impeccable. In *South Ward Grade School*, for example, Joe's description of the incident with Glenda Cook and her dad, Bill, matches mine exactly. Poor innocent Joe was just the tagalong. Bailey and I were the culprits. Well, I was the culprit. Yes, cowered up on this roof of a walkway that connected the original brick school with a tin quonset hut brought in to house the Boomer overflow, we all three were threatened by an angry father with placement in a juvenile facility.

Joe left Tuscola in 1965 for study at the University of Idaho, a career in forestry, and a marriage on the rim of the Grand Canyon to a California blond named Katherine. He never came back, and lives today on the "top" of a mountain in Western Colorado.

I never left Tuscola. But yet, when I read his essays, I realize Joe never left either. I stayed home for many reasons: parents, friends, career. In my most introspective moments, I sense I also stayed to freeze time, to never let go of those life-sustaining, life-enriching memories, to try to constantly loop those times over and over and over, so that I wouldn't forget, wouldn't get old, and my parents and sister and loved ones wouldn't die.

The Tuscola Joe left is no more—it has irrevocably changed—Joe and I agree on that. But the Tuscola of his memory is forever. It's forever because he has committed it to memory in this collection of essays. He makes the time and place of our youth come alive for me. What a wonderful gift for his classmates, the memory of his parents, and for Tuscola—its collective memory; its message to current citizens; its contribution to the town's dynamic and still unfolding communal story.

And what a gift for every person who has warm and rich memories of their growing up in any small American town during the middle of the 20th century, where we felt safe, enfolded by everyone in town like a third sheltering parent, when time seemed to stand still, life seemed to make sense, and was rewarding and full of purpose.

Thomas Wolfe said in 1940 "You Can't Go Home Again." But when I read Joe's essays I am almost there: I can see it clearly, almost feel, smell and taste it, even sense that if I just reach out a little, I can touch it. I am transported to a small slice of a special place and time.

—Mike Carroll
Tuscola, Illinois, May 2020

Author's Invitation

THIS BOOK IS about going home. It is about a place and a time that no longer exist—other than in my mind and my memory. The place is a small town in east-central Illinois. The time is mid-twentieth century—the 1950's and early 1960's. Tuscola was surrounded by corn and soybean fields on the black-soil prairie land common in mid-America. The time has long faded into years and decades. The place is still there, but the world surrounding it has changed beyond recognition.

What happened to the world of yesterday? When we were young and full of dreams—full of anticipation of a future still over the horizon? A future soon to become a past we yearn for.

Although I write this from my perspective, I want it to reflect a place and a time recognizable to any reader. I want others to say, "I remember a time or place similar to that." We all have hometowns and places where we grew up. Some of us stayed there, some of us left. Some of these places were small towns, some rural areas, some big cities. But most contained family and friends, neighborhoods and places that formed us and our values.

I came along about a century after Tuscola was founded, thus there are nearly 100 years' worth of Tuscola I never experienced. My time was a brief 18 years, the first 6 of which I have little recollection or consciousness of anything. So in the scheme of things, I viewed and experienced only a snapshot of Tuscola, but it was my hometown and that puts a stamp of ownership, pride, and interest.

I am writing this from a distant viewpoint. I look back over seventy summers of heat and thunderstorms, seventy autumns of vermillion- and gold-shaded streets, seventy winters of blizzards and bone-chilling cold, and seventy years of spring-time hope and rebirth. All add up to a lifetime of discovery, adventure, making mistakes, and finding meaning. Now, in the approaching winter of my life, I look for wisdom and knowledge worth passing on. I look for a legacy that sums up what it was all about. For all that, I search the past.

I began writing essays about Tuscola over thirty years ago—simply to capture important memories of my hometown and childhood—in order to remember them. Over the years, I kept adding, revising, deleting until it became a deeper, larger, story. With the passing of time, class reunions, the loss of parents, and even the passing of old friends and classmates, I decided to make more of this than just a collection of memories.

But what would it be? About my remembrances? No. I want it to be more than me, more than a small town. I want others from other places and backgrounds to be able to relate to similar situations. Yes, in remembering things from a place and time long ago, I focus on my childhood and my hometown. But it could also be about anyone and anyplace with similar memories of a hometown, a community where we knew our neighbors and shared lives and stories. As we grow into and past our prime, we focus on what we learned in life, especially childhood. We figure out the importance of large and small events of everyday life. My theme became the meaning of legacy, values, and lessons from our past.

Thus, this became a story of a place and a time now gone. Time changes and modifies the past, creating new begin-nings. Our lives develop as we sculpt who we are from all we learned. As we age, we put more value on that part of our lives that has disappeared. Soon, we watch our grandchildren and great-grandchildren experience similar things. Times and people change, technology changes, but much stays the same, with only details different.

What is a place and a time? There is more to a historic place than the fixtures and furniture, the pictures on the wall and the tile on the floor. The time is the attitude, the context of what is happening, the daily gossip and news discussed. It is the weekly fate of the football or basketball teams, the weather and the success of this year's corn crop, and who died the week before. It lives and changes from day-to-day, and tomorrow it is gone. There is no present. The future immediately becomes the past. We look forward to tomorrow and suddenly it is yesterday. You think about it late at night and occasionally share it at class reunions with others who were there but who probably haven't thought about it for years. Life passes by and the child you grew up with is now gone forever and you are left to witness life without that companion. Memories keep that life alive, but barely. It is the soul and conscience of each of us. Unlike a museum, it must be tasted and touched, but it is delicate and must be cared for with fragile concern.

Conscience must have values. My generation had values given us by the generation that sailed the Pacific dodging Kami-kazes, and marched across Italy or France dodging German Panzers—a generation hardened on the Great Depression and struggles and hardships that our generation would only read about. We had the values imparted on us by our parents and by our hometown as a whole.

So this book is about one person's reflections of the place and time where I grew up. My childhood and my life were different than others. I will remember some things but forget many things others do remember. I am not trying to create a history or a full remembrance of a town and its people. Each of us carries within us a story and each is different. I am recalling a time that from today's perspective, seemed very simple and good. The place where—in the black fertile soil—roots grow deep.

Tuscola, in the 1950s and '60s, was mine and always will be. Memory of course usually paints a picture in brighter colors than occurred. Childhood does the same thing. A hometown is made of memories of a childhood.

I invite you to join me on a journey of recollection of this place and time that has disappeared as surely as the buffalo and bluestem prairies. If I cause a smile, that is fine. If I cause a tear of sadness, that is fine as well. Smiles of happy memories are usually nourished by tears of remembrance and fondness of something that has disappeared in the mists of time.

❧

Caution—A Note on Memory

As I assembled this collection of essays, I realized a very important caveat: memory is an interesting phenomenon. I do not intend this to be a history, but mainly a reminiscence of some of my experiences and a generalized reflection of a place and a time. Our memories are a part of each of us and they are unique. Memories can be wrong, incomplete, or biased. We tend to forget bad memories, we enhance the good memories, and we mix up people, places, and times. I plead guilty to all of the above. But it really isn't important if I don't remember exactly how many classrooms were in the old North Ward or how many cornet players were in the high school band. Memories depend on many factors and reflect our conscious or unconscious biases and personalities. Looking back sixty-plus years, I remember some facts, and have forgotten many others. Details fade with time, and the importance of details fades as well. I want to capture the big picture, the meaning of a place, and my time in that place. So forgive me if my memory doesn't match that of my contemporaries in that place and time. If I can get you to say "I remember Ervin Park," or "my town was different but we had a similar park or theater," then I have succeeded. The world I am describing has disappeared but we all need to remember what long ago turned into yesterday.

PART I

҉

A Place: Hometown

A hometown is where dreams are formed and memories end. You may physically leave, move to new towns and begin new lives, but your hometown never leaves you. No matter where your life takes you on the many twists and turns of an unpredictable journey, you will always remember the place you grew up. Your hometown stamps the indelible image of houses, streets, businesses, schools, and people. It is a refuge where you are always welcome, if only in your memories. If you stay in your hometown, you become part of the living quilt of history.

ONE

LEAVING TUSCOLA

IT WAS MID-MORNING on a warm June day in 1965 when I climbed into Tim Lemna's black 1946 Ford in front of my house on E.N. Central Avenue. Tim and I drove off as I waved to my mom, standing in the doorway holding back tears. Tim and I planned this trip out west as our high school graduation present to ourselves. Sharing the same birthday, we were soon to share an experience of a lifetime. It was symbolic, but as we drove off, I certainly didn't think about what it all might mean.

Tim drove one block to Main Street, then turned south for one-half mile—past the old maples and elms of South Main—to the highway. He then turned right onto US Route 36, down under the US 45 overpass, then west across miles of endless prairie. We were on our way. We religiously stayed on that highway until the outskirts of Denver several days later. We camped out; we explored Rocky Mountain National Park, and the South Dakota Black Hills. I tasted my first beer at Tulagi's on the Hill in Boulder. We hiked with newfound female friends on the Bear Lake Trail in Rocky Mountain National Park, rented motorcycles in Estes Park, and watched *Cat Ballou* starring new actress Jane Fonda. We discovered a world different from our small hometown on the Illinois prairie.

Only later did I try to fathom meaning in this first major trip away from my hometown. This memoir is about what I now see as the values and the importance of a hometown and a childhood. How does a childhood hometown affect the rest of your life? Part of its importance is about the innocence and lifestyle now gone. It's about early friends and schoolmates who may stay with you for the rest of your life. For some, it's about leaving and remembering. For those who stayed, it's about seeing your world slowly change around you. It's about time travel and growing up and reaching for dreams while holding onto memories.

For me, it's about a small town and the surrounding farm-lands of central Illinois, and the values and horizons they imprinted on me. The flatness and lack of anything wild were what drove my desire to leave. I needed mountains and for-ests and the taste of freedom of the West. Only after years of breath-taking vistas and endless plains and mountains would I realize the subtle beauty, and the haunting simplicity of the fertile homeland I left years before.

I did not understand all that at the time—as Tim and I headed West—since I was focused on my upcoming major change of life: studying forestry in Idaho. Others in the Tuscola High School class of '65 were facing that same experience. Don took his basketball and a scholarship to Regis College in Den-ver, and Mike took his to Milliken in Decatur. Anne, Sharon, and Kathleen wore their white nurses' uniforms in schools in St. Charles, Springfield, and Champaign. And Mike and Mike slogged through boot camps, choosing a military life. Max and Carol stood on campuses in Bloomington-Normal, and Donna and Jackie, Shirley and Bob stayed in Tuscola with new careers but in familiar surroundings. We, and all our classmates, began to meet new challenges either in new places, far from home, or near home.

So the summer of 1965 was about leaving the comfort and safety of my hometown. I was ready to leave, so I had no sad feelings as we drove west that June. This was more than an adventure for me. It was a preview as well as a goodbye.

Only after years of reflection did I realize that the corn-fields and endless expanses of flatness—broken only by farm-houses and silos, red barns and railroad tracks—hold a beauty

I thought I could find only in snowcapped mountains and whitewater rivers. The black prairie soil holds onto your soul as surely as it holds onto the probing roots of oaks and sycamores along the river bottoms. The starkness of the winter landscape, where snowy ground merges into grey cloudy sky, fuses the landscape into a dizzying quilt that extends to the heavens. Its simplicity is full of a richness you have to squint to see. When it comes into view, it holds onto you.

For me, Tuscola will forever be the Fifties and early Sixties of the twentieth century. It ended in 1965 and will never change. Of course, I have witnessed physical changes, such as the burning down of the old Strand Theater, the tearing down of the South Ward School, the new subdivisions, and the new schools. But they might as well be in any other small town in America. They are not in the Tuscola of my mind and my experience. This is a wonderful gift, being able to travel back in time, but it does have its drawbacks. I am trapped by memory. I lead a double life: I live my dream of exploring new worlds; and live in memories of the days I spent in carefree childhood, with people and places never changing.

When I did return to Tuscola on visits to my folks', my time-travel would kick in. I could walk by houses nearly 40 years old in a typical residential neighborhood, but see only the old North Ward school that once stood there. I see Mrs. Prescott, my first-grade teacher. She seemed ancient in 1953, but then, to a six-year-old, I imagine most adults seem ancient. I hear old Mr. Taylor, the janitor of the original North Ward, and smell the musty basement where he scolded us to take off the galoshes our mothers made us wear in the winter slush. Tough love is not a new invention. I stand by the expanse of the playground at the new North Ward—the old high school—and remember the time the adjacent Brookside restaurant exploded.

I stand downtown on Sale Street and hear the clink of billiard balls in the pool hall, next to Nick's. Nick made his own chocolates, but I don't remember eating any; they were likely out of my price range then. I taste the suicide phosphate and hamburger that Gus Flesor made for me in Gus's, right there on the corner of Sale and Main Streets. Gus was a Tuscola institution—epitomizing the soda fountain-grill of small towns across America. Gruff and cantankerous, he always gave a little extra in your servings.

I visualize the new Allison's TV and Radio store on Route 36. The Allison's lived upstairs above the store. This caused a change in my life since Jimmy was one of my first childhood playmates; they had lived a few houses east of us, and my early photo albums are full of pictures of me and Jimmy and our proud mothers and older brothers.

None of these exist anymore. Not the old North Ward, nor the Ben Franklin where I worked as a stockboy, not Gus, not Brookside. And more importantly, not my mom or my dad. The house where I grew up belongs to new owners, strangers who cannot see and hear the spirits of that old place. These places and people have all been gone for years.

Why do I remember these things? Part of it is obviously to hold onto a youth long gone. But more significantly, they are part of the series of events and people that made me and my generation who we are. They include teachers, role models and mentors who helped form the values that grew in small rural towns of mid-century America. They are building blocks of trust, right and wrong, loyalty, pride, humility, honesty, and the hundred other things that we think about much later in life. When those teachers, parents, and heroes have left this earth, we are on our own. We then think about who we are and what we have done. That's when our peers become important, for these were kids we started life with, and all learned together. Most of us learned very well and share these basic values. More importantly, we inherited the roles of mentor, teacher, hero.

Only later did I realize the value and importance of things like the Strand Theater, Little League Yankees, the Community Building and Teen Town dances, and high school Study Hall.

I thank my mother for the ritual of taking my class picture every year from first grade through eighth on my birthday at the end of May. I look at the high school yearbook, and those pictures of me and my classmates standing in front of our grade school teachers: Nellie Prescott, Rita Roderick, Bess Bundy, Juanita Michener, Marguerite McDaniel, Elmer Broyles, Janet Southard. I try to think about why those pictures are important. Then I realize they are important to me because they were my life in a place and time.

⁓

Memories are too important to lose—so what better way to begin this collection than to think back on those days Tim and I cruised Route 36 through Missouri and Kansas. And think about what I was looking forward to in a new life out West, and what I was leaving behind frozen in time in Tuscola, Illinois, 1965.

TWO

HOMETOWN

EVERYONE HAS A hometown, whether a large or small city, small town or a rural community. A hometown can be where you were born and lived throughout childhood. It can also be a town you moved to early in life. It is a place that takes you in, wraps you tightly in its history and its present, hoping for a future. It is where your home and family are and where you have your friends and most importantly, your memories of growing up. You spend time playing, laughing, crying, studying, worshiping. You know your neighbors' names. You can go into a store and the clerk knows your name. Because we didn't have dial phones during my time, you could pick up the phone and the operator would say hi and ask how you and your parents were doing. Hometown will forever be the place where you can return if only in your memory, to feel safe, where you belong. It is where you enjoyed the freedom of childhood and where you struggled in adolescence to reach maturity.

Tuscola, Illinois, is my hometown. The place was special, but just as important, the time was as well. My time there involved the magical period mid-twentieth century, when life was good and getting better, at least for a small town in rural mid-America. The distant past of this small town—foreign to me, but brought to life daily through my parents and the elders of the town—hung on with tenacity, transferring the good values from parents, teachers and mentors, and hiding the evil that lurked somewhere else, outside the hometown. The time and the town were my "growing up" experience.

Tuscola is a small town in east-central Illinois, tucked amid endless rectangular corn and soybean fields. Thousands of years ago, it was covered with vast glaciers, moving northern prairies' rich topsoil and depositing it where the thickness of the black humus is now measured in feet, hiding the limestone of former seas, and diverse and rich biology and human history.

About one-mile square, the town was bordered by two major highways and three railroads. Only two highways existed while I lived there, the third—Interstate 57—was constructed about the time I left home. Route 45—running alongside and west of the railroad bypassing town—led north to Champaign-Urbana and the campus of the University of Illinois, then northwards to the magical but mysterious metropolis of Chicago, home of the Cubs and wondrous museums. South led to the football rival Arcola, my dad's home place in rural Effingham County, and eventually Mobile, and the Gulf coast. Highway 36—stretching from sunrise to sunset, including distant Denver and the Rocky Mountains—paralleled the south side of town, although several housing developments were oozing south of the road. East was a seldom-traveled path to Indianapolis and beyond. There were few reasons for me to go south or east while I lived in Tuscola, and northern trips rarely went beyond Champaign.

With a population of somewhere around four thousand, plus the larger farming community surrounding it, everybody generally knew everybody else, including all the warts and gossip that comes with the territory. Even though the two east-west railroads ran through the middle of town, it was hard to identify a right and wrong side of the tracks. Many of the wealthier and prosperous town fathers lived south of the tracks, and the Douglas County Courthouse is located there, but two of the three schools, the hospital, several churches, and the business district were north of the tracks. The north-south

Illinois Central tracks on the west side of town didn't count in this symbolism. Several businesses lined Highway 36, but this was so far from my house, it barely existed.

༃

As with most baby boomers born in 1947 in Tuscola, I entered life in Jarman Hospital. An old brick building, it was the pride of a small town; now long reduced to dust, its newer wing was renovated as an apartment complex. Modern towns the size of Tuscola can never again support a full-service hospital, but back then, it was our life saver. My generation was called Jarman babies and that in itself bonds us forever.

Since I didn't learn to ride a bicycle until the fourth grade, my world was limited to a few blocks. I simply didn't need to go further than this. Grade schools were within walking distance. We usually walked to church, a "long" hike of three blocks. Another block or two past that was Dr. Boylson's office, our family physician. You were classified by several things in town: what school you went to (south of the tracks went to the South Ward, I went to the North Ward), what church you belonged to, and who your doctor was.

Being "old-timers," my folks could relate the early years of Tuscola, although they were far from being town fathers or mothers. Tuscola had been around since the days of neighbor Abe Lincoln and early photos amazed me of the changes the little town had seen. Tuscola had weathered the Depression; both world wars; and the Civil War, too—as it wasn't very far south of Tuscola you had to travel to reach rural areas of Illinois that favored Jeff Davis. But all that was very ancient history, mostly forgotten by my time.

There were few strangers in town. By either personal knowledge or reputation, we knew most people. Or at least those of importance and worth knowing. It helped that my folks had lived in this town for over thirty years. They were married in 1934 in the house I grew up in, and were active in church, which their lives revolved around. Dad was born and lived in Effingham County, sixty miles south, but in the early twenties had come to Tuscola to attend his senior year of high school. He taught in a one-room school for a few years in his hometown but then moved to Tuscola in the late twenties to work at the Corn Belt Building and Loan on Sale Street. Dad was the secretary and the moving force of the Corn Belt. He and his brother Clyde were the only employees I ever knew, so most people called it the Colwell Brothers Agency. They also sold insurance, so they were a mainstay of the town. Whenever I see the movie *It's a Wonderful Life*, I equate the Jimmy Stewart character with my dad. Throughout my life, I heard stories from people who would tell how Dad gave them a loan to buy their first house, often when no one else would loan them money. He never bragged about any of this; it was just part of his job. He remained at the Corn Belt when it merged with another savings and loan, and he retired before that S&L went belly up along with others in the bank crises of the 1980s. Dad was a Mason, but I don't think he ever attended the Lodge in Tuscola. He was an avid coon hunter, and would spend many winter evenings hunting with his coon-dog-owning buddies, Bruce Williams and Bill Daniel. He didn't care about keeping the coon skins—he was in it for the joy of hunting. And the joy of trying to outwit raccoons.

Mom was born in Newman, Illinois, and her family moved to the edge of Tuscola when she was a little girl, so she essentially grew up here. Mom was always working in either the Ben Franklin, Four Seasons, or Carpenters Clothing stores. Before my memory kicked in, she worked at the Star Store and rode a bicycle around town selling silverware. However, all social life revolved around Eastern Star (including being Grand Matron)

and later, DeMolay Mothers. Mom would occasionally host bunco club, whatever that was; all I knew was that several ladies would come over in the evening, Dad would disappear coon hunting, and I hid in the kitchen or my room, sneaking down and eavesdropping on gossip I never thought interesting.

Even though we weren't part of the social scene of the town, my folks were considered a solid part of Tuscola's history. Mom was the very first Miss Tuscola, winning the contest in a borrowed man's bathing suit, being too poor to own a woman's suit. Of course, in those days of the early Depression, a man's suit was not much different than a woman's and covered all aspects of decency. At any rate, this fact was generally little known and not part of my growing up. A Mom is a mom and a six-year-old boy certainly doesn't think of his mother as a beauty queen.

Since my brother is six years older than me, he was off to college by the time I was in seventh grade, and memory being what it was for me, I don't remember many details about him when I was little. I was always a straight-A student; though, in the early grades, excellence was marked as an E, for excellent; and F was still an F and I do not remember what came in between. I rarely earned anything less than an E or later an A so I paid it no mind.

Being part of the older generation that I never understood at the time, my folks were not my pals or close friends, as modern parents seem to be. All my grandparents were dead either before I was born or soon thereafter, thus I missed out knowing any earlier generations. It was hard to be a friend of a father who was 52 years old by the time I was old enough to play Little League or go camping. I don't ever remember having an adult conversation with either of them while I lived at home. Unfortunately, Mom passed on before I heard her old age recollections of her life, but Dad related his stories to me many times. I always listened politely, until I can almost recite them myself.

✌

Hometown means knowing most of the town fathers, mothers, drunks, and other assorted subjects of intense gossip, which in all hometowns is usually a favorite pastime. For example, Freddie Jones, owner of the Hotel Douglas, was usually seen with a big cigar in his mouth, but rarely seen sober. At least that was his reputation, true or not. Inherited from his parents, the hotel was an elegant staple of this small town. It was built in 1899 and destroyed by fire in 1975; during my time it housed Fred Cooch and Paul Roderick's barbershop, which I frequented on Saturday mornings, right after depositing my paper route money in the bank across the street. The images and the smell of the barbershop cologne still rattle in my olfactory brain memory—like an old Norman Rockwell painting. I can visualize the linoleum floor, the large mirrors behind the two (or was it three?) barber chairs, the bottles of cologne lining the glass shelves in front of the mirrors, the stacks of *Saturday Evening Post* along with the *Superman* comic books. But the description does no justice to the memory; I also remember the ambiance, the feeling, my emotions as a ten-year-old boy, and the pace of life in this mid-century, mid-America small town.

One characteristic of a small town, and possibly of neighborhoods in larger towns as well, is the familial relationships. Many people are related, with a plethora of siblings, cousins, aunts, uncles, and grandparents. Thus gossip gets chancy since you have to be careful who you are talking about because it may be a relation of the person you are talking to. For example, Albrittons were related to Seips, Koehnemanns to Hubers, Webers to Webers, Carrolls to McGuires, and who could tell about Kleiss, Kappes, Rahn, or Little. This, of course, didn't stop gossip.

The extended families were woven through the community life, like the weft and warp of a tapestry. However, this changed a little in the early '50s when the large chemical company we called Petro chose the valuable farmland west of town to build a huge petrochemical plant. Whether Petro was really its name or we just called it that—it was known later as USI—it brought an influx of newcomers which included a lot of high paying engineering jobs as well as kids my age. New blood always changes a community and it did Tuscola. My grade school class increased enough to add a new teacher.

～

My hometown was pretty much self-contained, even with its relatively small population. We had doctors, a hospital, grocery stores, furniture stores, clothing stores, a five and dime, three lumber yards, the post office, a library, schools, and churches. Most businesses were downtown, where I felt they belonged. After I left for college was when downtown businesses either went out of business or migrated to the south edge of town, along the highway. What more you got by going to the big city was not well understood by me. Of course, Champaign-Urbana had the university, which was a big deal, especially when my brother studied there. But other than having more of every-thing, why go there? It did have an eye doctor, which I visited regularly, being genetically inclined to very poor vision. And it did have the TV station (WCIA), which on one big occasion, I visited the live afternoon show with Captain Eddie. And it also had the Hop, the dance show that the high schoolers drooled over, but that of course never interested me.

Two staples of any hometown, if it is large enough, are the library and the post office. Tuscola is blessed with memorable examples of each. The library is a genuine Carnegie, old enough in my early days to be an institution of classic elegance. It is stone-faced, with pillars embellishing the magnificent stone steps and façade. Those were the days of public buildings pre-ADA ramps or elevators. I never saw anyone in a wheelchair in town, much less needing help to get up the many steps into the library, churches, or schools. That all came later, buildings in mid-century were made for able-bodied folks. The library had a wood counter that greeted patrons. Off to the left were the books and the study room with a large table. To the right was the more comfortable reading room with overstuffed chairs, couches, and a large fireplace. There were more stacks downstairs, but my use of the library was limited to the room with the encyclopedias and other reference books. I probably checked out books, but early in life, I started the habit of buying the books I was interested in and have continued that all my life. Many school evenings, the smaller study room was filled with the different cliques, engaged in faux study, but mainly in real gossip. I felt out of place, so rarely visited in the evenings.

The post office is next to the library and was built during the Great Depression. I have since seen several other small-town post offices that are copy-cat designs of Tuscola's building. You enter a small foyer with two doors going into the main lobby. The boxes line the walls, and the counters were faced with the cage bars that meant the desk was closed. There was a door marked Postmaster, which in our case was Wayne Neal or Milas Thomas. Covering one wall to the ceiling was a Depression-era mural of a farm scene and horse-drawn wagon. It is still there. I may have spent more time in the post office than I did the library, but found both fascinating.

The other staple of Tuscola is the courthouse, built in 1913, being the third courthouse since the County was organized in 1859. Being the county seat, we were a step above neighboring Arcola, Arthur, Atwood, Newman, and Villa Grove. We had the magnificent stone building sitting smack in the center of a whole city block. But some mix-up decades before put this center of activity not downtown—as in many other small county seats, with the main business district surrounding the courthouse square—but two blocks south of the railroad tracks and three blocks south of the business district. Rumors explained this a couple of ways, but the accepted one was the railroad was supposed to be located a few blocks away from where it was actually built. It seems a lame excuse, but whatever reason, the courthouse is located in a residential area south of the tracks. I thought it added a peacefulness that would not have been found if surrounded by a business district.

A hometown elicits pride. No matter what a person may like or dislike about the hometown: just like an ugly dog, it's yours and no one else dares make fun of it. This pride usually surfaces in the school sports teams. You may have the worst football or basketball team in the conference, but no one but you can admit it. The only thing I knew about the high school teams before I was in high school, was they usually played their football games on Friday afternoon (before lights allowed night games). I didn't know anyone in high school (other than my brother, who as a sibling didn't count) and the only thing I knew about sports was everyone in Tuscola hated Arcola. In those days, the sports consisted of basketball and football. There was track, but that was not exactly a spectator sport. Girls were left out unless they wanted to be cheerleaders or pom-pom girls. Being much too small and uncoordinated to play any sport, I was relegated to being in the marching band.

In later years, I lived in or near many other small towns. I tried to take an interest in the people, the history, the politics, but I never belonged in the way I did in Tuscola. There is only one hometown and if you are lucky, you are born into it or move early in life and you are part of it as you grow and it becomes part of you.

THREE

HOME

$\mathbf{M}$OST OF US have a house we grew up in. Some may have had more than one, possibly in more than one town. But whether one or more, there was usually only one house that was home, a safe haven that provided security and comfort to us when we were very young. It was the base of operations for our wandering and playing, which most often spread all over town. If we were lucky, home was on a farm or ranch where we could wander unhindered. It was safe in those days and we often were gone all day on bicycles or with neighbor friends. Our parents didn't worry—it was the '50s after all.

Home was where we played with toy soldiers or hid from the dragon. It was where we played with the dolls around the tea set or became the fairy princess. Our imagination made our home into a castle or Wild West fort. Our friends came for sleepovers, often in a tent in the yard. We played tag, hide and seek, and found nightcrawlers floating on the lawn after summer thunderstorms. Home was peaceful, safe, and always there.

～

My home was 204 E.N. Central. I always thought the East North was a little pretentious and unnecessary. North Central and South Central Avenues are parallel to the east-west railroad tracks. And there is only one block west of Main Street, so most houses were East.

We lived smack in the middle of town: one block to the Post Office; two blocks to downtown, where Dad worked and where all the shopping was centered; three blocks to church; one or two blocks to several grocery stores, as well as schools. What else would anyone need?

On the other side of the street in front of the house were the railroad tracks, and this provided endless hours of watching trains, putting rocks on the rail and then throwing other rocks at them to knock them off. I was Audie Murphy shooting the Japs or Krauts or whoever the bad guys were that day. I made sure to knock all the rocks off since I didn't want to derail any trains. I did leave pennies on the rails, though. I probably flattened a small fortune, thinking what a neat consequence of the theory of gravity and mass. It wasn't enough to push me into a profession of physics, but the flattened and distorted Abe Lincoln really impressed me. I did give an occasional worry that the thickness of the penny just might be enough to derail a speeding train, but that never happened. I guess my childhood was lucky indeed. A derailed train right across the street from my house might destroy my home, or at least lead the railroad cops to deduce just who caused the wreck. My mind was working all right, I figured, if I thought of all these potential consequences. I spent a lot of time by myself thinking and daydreaming.

I heard rumors that our house was one of the first built in the new village of Tuscola in the mid-1860s. Others said "of course not." To me, that didn't matter. Something that old was ancient history. I didn't want to live in ancient history. That was certainly not cool. What was cool was that the house was my home. For eighteen years, it was the only home I ever knew. Small and simple, and yes, old, it sits across the street from the railroad tracks, and when it was built that was status since it was only two blocks from the center of town. I found no status in that—by my time the town center was moving south.

Living across the street from the east-west railroads, trains of the Baltimore and Ohio and the C&EI Railroads roared by several times a day, shaking the windows in the house and irritating us with the incessant blaring of horns and idling locomotives day and night. We decided early in life the engineers delighted in the thought they would awaken us all night long with their cacophony.

ॐ

On a warm April day in 2002, I sat in my rented U-Haul truck parked in front of 204 E. N. Central. I looked at that old house one last time. I had helped rip the heart out of it, emptying it of its soul as my brother and I spent a week sorting through, tossing out what had no value to us or anyone else, picking the few items we wanted to save, and packing the rental truck. Dad had died the month before, Mom eight years before that. They were married in that house in 1934, right after Dad bought it for a little less than $2000. They lived in it together, then Dad by himself, for nearly 68 years. Nowhere else in that long span of time was there any other home for them. Or for me, although I had moved my life elsewhere almost 40 years earlier.

But I couldn't keep this now empty house, nor could my brother. It was our house to grow up in, and it was the house our parents grew old in. It was theirs and since they were now gone, we had to let go. After an auction to sell the things we couldn't take, the house would be sold. I said my goodbyes as I walked the now-empty rooms, and slept the last time forever in my bedroom of youth. While my brother drove to Champaign to meet his son at the airport, I chose that moment to drive away for the last time. Forever. That seven-letter word kept coming to my mind. My parents were gone forever. My home would now be gone forever. I was leaving my Tuscola home for the last time. Forever. I turned my head, wiped my eyes, and put the truck in drive and I didn't look back.

But the long drive across the cornfields of Illinois and Iowa, the unending prairies of Kansas and Colorado, and the spine of the Colorado Rockies, gave me ample time to revisit what 204 E. N. Central meant to me. I took old Route 36 to Denver, the same route we traveled to visit Aunt Mabel and Uncle Chuck when they lived in Boulder. Those visits turned my dreams from boring flat Illinois cornfields to the mountains.

Now, as I study the scant collection of family photos, I see I was born before the enclosing of the front porch. I was born before an old coal shed out by the alley was torn down. I can remember the old gas floor furnaces that were under the house. The floor grates, large enough to lay on during cold winter mornings, one in the front room, one in the dining room, helped heat the entire house. If I dig through the cobwebs of memory, I can envision other things of my very early childhood, but dig deeply I must. Some things that have always been there are hard to see clearly. They were just there. Sort of like the sky and summer thunderstorms, and cloudy, dreary November days.

I don't remember anything of those early years before I entered grade school. I am envious of people who can relate memories of being a two- or four-year-old. My memory is a total blank with only an exception or two. I do remember walking down East Sale Street to my first day of kindergarten. In those days, this was a private school since kindergarten was not part of the public school system. Those were the early Fifties and at least the earliest education came only to those with privilege. My folks thought I deserved this privilege, but I had different ideas. The school, in Mrs. Vest's house on Sale Street, was only about five blocks away from my house. I remember walking this long tree-lined street, but it seemed to be a trip to a different world. I'm sure my folks walked me there ahead of time as practice, but I was on my own for that first day. Parents trusted kids in those peaceful days. That level of responsibility followed me in later days.

I found the actual school a total waste of time. I have no

idea what we did other than nap time. Of course, I only gave it one or two days; my impatience was early to blossom. To my young inquiring mind, walking down this endless street so I could lay on the floor and pretend to nap was the height of stupidity. If this was what education was all about, I was in the wrong profession. I told my parents I wasn't going back. And I didn't. I do vividly remember the consequences. I was confined to bed for at least one day. But I got my way. I couldn't read (would I have learned that in napping kindergarten?) so I spent all day of my punishment perusing a *Mighty Mouse* comic book. Of course, my reading involved looking at pictures and wondering what all those words meant. I guess I had faith that on my own, I would pick up minor details of education like reading. I guess I got past that since I soon filled my bedroom walls with books, most purchased from the Weekly Reader Book Club. That proved that slow starters could certainly catch up and not be burdened by being obstinate.

For my first five years, my bed was still a crib in my parents' bedroom. This is rather embarrassing to think of now, but my five-year-old mind didn't comprehend those subtleties of life. We had a modest-size house, and the downstairs bedroom was rented to Orson Moorehead, the town cop. This helped my folks earn a few dollars. My entrance into this life was not enough of a jolt to oust Orson. A crib in my parents' room seemed all right to them. My older brother Ron got the other small bedroom upstairs. One would think—and for years I certainly wondered—that after a year or two, I would bump Ron downstairs to the bigger bedroom and I would inherit his small room. It happened, but only after my non-kindergarten experience.

When I left for college, Mom claimed my old room and stored my books and LP collection in the drawers of the built-in bookcase/desk that Earl Busby made for me when I entered high school; Earl was a carpenter and one of Dad's pheasant-hunting buddies. I dismantled the desk-bookcase, and it came home with me on that April day in 2002; it is where I now work at my computer writing essays and fiction. Also on that rental truck were the buffet and dining room table and chair set that were my folks' first pieces of furniture in 1934.

࿔

The entire backyard was a garden. I did have a side yard to play in, but that was taken over by garage and driveway after I left for college. During my time, we rented one stall in Clara Bruhn's two-car garage, two houses to the east. When Clara died, Dad had the choice of parking out front along the street or destroying the side yard. The backyard, which to many would have been the logical choice for building a garage, was off-limits. That garden had been carefully tended for too many decades to be paved over.

The week in April 2002 that I stayed alone in the house—empty of the life-long inhabitants, but still full of possessions—I was a stranger learning the secret lives of two people, never mind they were my parents. I was discovering details of their lives, which didn't belong to me. I belonged to them, but in this case, the reverse cannot be claimed. This is a phenomenon most people go through at some point. A child is always part of them, but the parent isn't part of the child except in a distant way. They create the child, raise him, instill values, then push the bird out of the nest. They had a life before I came along. I now was able to glimpse part of that.

In my explorations while in the house alone—before my brother arrived each day from his own home, one hour distant, to help do the sorting and cleaning—I discovered the attic, which I never knew existed. This was a narrow walkway between the upstairs rooms and the steeply slanted roof. There was barely room to walk, but I found how to get there on both sides of the upstairs. On one side, I discovered an old baby buggy, most likely not mine, but something Mom picked up

20

somewhere. On the other, through the closet in their bedroom, I found the old dog dish with Wiggle's name embossed on it, plus his old bed; I never knew they had saved those. We lost Wiggles when I was still in grade school. A Heinz-57-variety mutt, he had wandered by one day when I was probably about 8 and stayed with us for several years. One time he didn't come home from his wanderings around town and we never saw him again. There is an old saying about a boy and his dog. Wiggles was my dog and I grew up with him and I loved him as only a boy can. I always wondered what happened to him but I will never know. I still miss him, as I miss the time he shared with us.

I found letters of condolence to my mother when her father died. That was before I was born. I found, buried deep in her cedar chest, the poem *Little Boy Blue*, by Eugene Field, that she had copied onto poster board when she was a schoolgirl. It still brings tears to my eyes. The whole time I was going through the stuff of their lives, I felt sad at times, curious at others. When I found that school project, the emotions flooded me like a tsunami. I lay on the floor—probably at the exact spot she and my father stood to be wed in 1934—and bawled like a baby. This was a person I never knew: my mother as a young girl. What child can possibly know a parent this way? We are not meant to and at times I almost wished I hadn't found that. But then, I know she would have smiled at the thought of my finding it; that she was smiling that April morning as she wiped away my tears, Dad standing by her with his hand on her shoulder.

Sitting in that empty shell of a house, lost in memories, I wondered about their dreams. These were two people I never really knew, but they started a life together in times that carried worries and fears I had never known. They came from simple families, tied to the land, and they created a life for themselves here in this house, the center of their life for over 60 years. What were their dreams? They didn't have the wanderlust I had. Or did they, secretly, dream of things they were not prepared to risk a life for? Were they happy here? Did their two sons fulfill their secret wishes? I would never know. They carried such dreams and secrets to their graves, now a part of this black Illinois soil they grew up on.

⌘

As I sat there getting ready to drive away, I thought about the idea of a home. For many of my far distant ancestors, there was no such thing. They carried their home with them or moved around following a food source. I thought about animals who don't have homes. The wild turkey chick breaks out of an egg, dries itself off quickly, waits for siblings to hatch out, then mom leads the brood off, walking and wandering. The deer fawn drops, stumbles around, then follows mom. The wolf pup has the comfort of a den under a rock or dug into the ground; but soon, she starts moving and doesn't stop until she has her own pups.

Depending on where my ancestors may have lived, whether the plains of ice age Europe or the warm shores of the Mediterranean, they may have had a cave or animal-skin hut. Home moved and rarely stayed the same. I had a luxury of modern living. I stayed in one place, savoring the familiar, the comfortable. I knew my neighbors, I came home each day to my own den where I could relax and feel safe. Many in this world have never had this feeling of safety. Does that give a person an advantage over another who must learn new places, challenge new dangers, overcome fear and the unknown? I had a home and it lasted much of my life, although most of that time, it was an idea and a knowledge that there always was a place where I grew up and learned what life was.

Nowadays, many people move around too frequently to develop the bond of place and time that I had. I've counted the times I moved in my adult life. No house or place holds or possibly could hold my memories and the life that 204 held for my parents. The house was not fancy, but it was their life, their safe place. It was mine also for a while, but I was only a visitor. Their home was mine but it was a part that could not be separated. Until it was no longer their home. That is when I lost it as my home. It was them, and held the secrets, the hopes, the happiness, the sadness of their lives from that day in 1934 they stood in the living room saying their wedding vows, until that day my widowed father fell on the ice on a cold winter Sunday and sealed his fate. Broken ribs, punctured lungs, and a life soon ended. That house will forever be their lives, even when it disappears and turns into a vacant lot I will never see—sometime in the distant haze of the future.

Do I get to come back sometime and relive those times? A time when as a small boy, I wait impatiently for Santa Claus on a late December morning? When on a cold January morning, I lay on the floor furnace warming my cold feet? A time I look down from my bed and listen to Wiggles snoring on his bed by my feet? A time we come back from midnight services at Southside Christian church and I look up in the night sky wondering if those were the same stars baby Jesus saw? A time on a bright May morning when I look out my bedroom window and see a garden full of red strawberries and I hurry downstairs so I can pick some to put on my cereal? A time as a little boy when I sneak into my mother's bed while Dad is still out coon hunting, then wake up when he gets home at midnight and carries me into my own bed. A time when as a Little League Yankee, I don my uniform and primp in front of the mirror, knowing my playing days will never live up to my dreams? A time when in late October, I dress up as a bum, with a cigar in my mouth as I head out for trick or treating, not worrying at all about what is placed in my sack?

The times were good for a boy growing up. And 204 E. N. Central was the center of my world. The house and its memories were like an island surrounded by an endless sea that was sinking fast and I knew I had to leave. I no longer belonged in my boyhood home. Saying goodbye to that house on that street on a sunny April day in 2002 also meant saying goodbye to a world long ago faded into memories that last and grow until we take the last breath we will ever take in this world, in a place we can only dream of.

FOUR

DOWNTOWN

My HOMETOWN WAS centered around the downtown. The corner of Main Street and Sale Street was ground zero: a bank on one corner; the big Hotel Douglas on one; Gus's on the southwest corner; and Anderson's drygoods on the other, with the cupola on top, and the five-and-dime next door.

During my time there, Tuscola was small but still had a lot to offer. We had Champaign or Decatur to go to if we needed a large town. Downtowns like Tuscola in the Fifties have mostly disappeared; the last I saw my downtown, it was dominated by vacant buildings or knick-knack souvenir shops. Most of the big shopping was south on Route 36, or else online.

The five-and-dime, whose proper name was Wellworths, had everything in it. I could not imagine needing anything not in that store. It was next to the telephone building, where real live operators sat to connect each and every phone call, years before direct dialing came to town.

A step up from the dime store was the Ben Franklin on Sale Street, across from the Strand Theater. That store played a significant part of my high school years since I worked there as a stockboy. I especially enjoyed checking the weekly top 20 chart from Chicago radio station WLS. It is where I bought my first record player and started my collection of Kingston Trio, Brothers Four, and other LPs. When manager Don Couch moved out to his own store called Four Seasons on Route 36, I followed him there after helping set up the Ben Franklin for new owner Jay Vincent and working there briefly as a stockboy before heading out to the Four Seasons. Don soon made the Four Seasons into strictly a clothing store, abandoning the few dime-store-type items he initially carried.

Almost everything was clustered in the one-block cross-section of Sale and Main Streets. The bank where I weekly obtained a money order for my paper route was on the prestigious corner. Another bank was one block south; I rarely went in there, but do vaguely remember the wood teller counter with the metal grate windows.

Hotel Douglas had a café in the basement and the barbershop on the ground floor. I don't ever remember going in the main lobby of the hotel, nor did I visit the café, but I do remember thinking it must be some exotic thing due to the name "café." That name sounded foreign to me so I assumed the café itself must be rather unusual. I remember noticing signs in the window advertising the "Blue Plate Specials." I had no idea what that was, but it sounded as exotic as "café."

To me, the centerpiece of downtown—other than the Strand Theater—was Gus's, a Tuscola institution. Along with hamburgers and home-made chocolates, he served old fashioned sodas at the fountain counter, where I imbibed many a suicide phosphate—all flavors mixed with the phosphate and fizz. Years later, when I worked at the University of Idaho Student Union, I introduced phosphates; they had never heard of such a drink. I wondered if it was a Midwestern thing since it seemed so common in my Tuscola youth.

Bert Quackenbush's *Tuscola Review* was down Sale Street half a block, soon to become Bob Hastings' and a Tuscola institution. I was the sports editor for Bob's rival *Tuscola Journal*, owned and edited by Phil White, another Tuscola institution, located across the alley and next to the new Community Building on West North Central Avenue. I remember Bob more as the coach of the Little League Indians, a rival of my Little League Yankees.

Downtown also contained Mitchell Cohen's clothing store, Jay North Furniture, and Aldridge Jewelry. And next to Rosies (how can I describe Rosies—"If you couldn't find it in Rosies, it didn't exist"), was the Corn Belt Building and Loan. I spent much time there since it was where my dad worked. When Dad had the front entrance to his building remodeled with flagstone steps, he had a silver dollar embedded in the mortar. It disappeared within a week. So much for the honesty of those "simpler" days.

Downtown Tuscola had about all you would need. The "Grab it Here" grocery was a block north of downtown, and there was a corner grocery on the west end of Sale Street. A Western Auto was north of the hotel and there were three lumber yards within a couple of blocks. Nick's was next to the pool hall. Nick's was started by Gus's brother years before and offered homemade chocolates. Carpenters Clothing competed with Mitchells and was on the first floor underneath the Masonic hall. On the eastern edge of the "main drag" was the Carnegie Library and the Post Office.

The era has disappeared where the downtown of a small town, or even larger towns, was the center of the community. The downtown I knew contained the main businesses of the community and nearly all were owned and operated by our neighbors. We seemed to have a focus then and our downtown was the center of that focus. We met our neighbors as we banked and shopped, got our prescriptions filled, even "traded" for groceries. Most businesses were glad to have schoolkids paint Halloween pictures on the windows. There was no other graffiti.

The downtown offered the comfort and neighborliness that has disappeared nowadays. We often hear the term "brick and mortar" stores. The internet and online shopping have destroyed the personal touch we found in stores owned by our neighbors. We could walk in, talk to the owner, touch and feel the items, try them on, sit in them, haggle for a better deal. I also never understood the desire to drive 25 miles to Champaign to get something a few dollars cheaper. Even with the inexpensive gas, why spend the time and money to save a dollar? "Shop local" meant more than economics; it also meant being neighbors and feeling part of a community.

❧

I could go back now and walk Sale and Main and most likely not know anyone. I know I have forgotten several businesses that others will remember. That is the sadness of an incomplete memory. But in the Fifties and Sixties, I "owned" those streets and that downtown.

FIVE

A School of Memories: Old North Ward Grade School

W E HAD NO such thing as middle school or junior high in the Tuscola school system. All first through eighth grade students attended grade school. When I started school in 1953, there were two different buildings—the old North Ward and the South Ward. All the grade schools that I attended have since been torn down and replaced. But my memories start with the old North Ward school.

Located in the half-block bounded by Ensey, Court, and Overton Streets, the old North Ward is only a memory and has been for over six decades. In an article by Lynnita Aldridge Brown for the *Tuscola Review* in 1986, my mother remembered the May Pole dances west of the building, the Halloween parties and Christmas. She also vividly remembers one Christmas when there was a barrel filled with gifts; before she was blind-folded, she spied an orange. Since an orange was a rare treat, she wanted that orange. She got it, making her Christmas special. She had other memories of having class under the trees. It could have been in this building she copied the poem that so touched me when I found it cleaning out the house in 2002.

When I read the article and recalled my own memories, I noticed the strange way that memory emphasizes what is important. My mind puts a high value on certain things although I'm still not sure why. The more times I unlock my memory, the more vivid the scenes appear. Maybe it is escape or nostalgia—longing for the good-old-days.

I remember the wide and quite grand (to an eight-year-old) wooden staircase heading up to the second floor. They served one purpose: to lead us into and out of the building—to learn, to play, to begin life. Maybe my most vivid vision is a late May afternoon: holding onto ancient traditions we'd shout, "school's out, school's out, teacher let the monkeys out." Somehow, those grand steps seemed proper to hop down, with the glorious school-free summer ahead of us, proudly proclaiming that we passed the second grade, and on to the next pinnacle—third grade. I don't know if modern second graders still chant that silly verse, but somehow it just wouldn't sound the same coming out of double glass doors of a sleek modern building.

I've driven or walked by the old place several times since the brick building was torn down and replaced by a block full of houses. They've been there long enough now that the maple and sycamore trees—well over a half-century old—make the block appear a permanent and mature residential neighborhood. Young adults will remember these houses as their homes the rest of their lives, unaware they were built over ghosts.

The old school building was rather stately if you can say that of a stodgy, square, two-story brick building, with large windows that must have been designed and used only for old schools. It certainly wasn't as impressive as the South Ward, or the old High School, both of which swept along for a full block, with gyms, cafeterias and the like. It had character in its simplicity. And it had that big field behind it. The one where we played football and chased each other for various reasons, sport, and non-sport. No baseball diamond, no track, no basketball hoops or soccer cage. Just an open grassy place where young minds made their own rules. A two-car garage with automatic door opener now stands as a tombstone on the spot where I learned one of those basic lessons of life—getting the wind knocked out of you when you end up with the football on the bottom of a pile of guys all bigger than you.

The jungle gym and swings were in the front of the building. Yes, there was a great jungle gym. I remember hanging upside down after getting my first pair of glasses and hearing the first taunts of "hey four eyes." The schoolyard was only three blocks from my house, but I don't remember playing there in the summer or on weekends. I only remember those times during school. Is my mind playing tricks or is this some kind of symbolism? Maybe the school itself is what I remember.

It's not important for me to know who built the school, or when, or even who the teachers were. They were all women and they were all old (aren't most adults old to an eight-year-old?). But it is important that I remember Mr. Taylor. He was the janitor and he looked after us, as grumpy old janitors do. He was grumpy because he cared for us and for this building. Of course, we did not appreciate him. He yelled at us when we tracked mud into the classrooms. I went over to his house one time (for what reason I have no idea, but I'm sure I was terrified) and remember that he was a real person with a friendly wife and real clothes other than the blue overalls he wore all the time. I figured out that there was a job requirement that all janitors, as well as teachers, look alike. They were also required to be grumpy to the kids, but once in a while, they let down their guard.

Like when I left my rubber overshoes in the basement coat room and my mother had to drag me back to retrieve them and I thought I actually saw him smile and wink at her. I'm sure Mr. Taylor understood. It was probably then I realized, but would not admit, that maybe he was a pretty nice old man after all. I doubt if I was the only kid that was forced to wear these overshoes by his mother, but I was embarrassed by having to be seen in public by the other kids that weren't forced to wear them. Thus the haste to shed the boots as soon as I got in the building and quickly hide them so as not to be seen wearing "momma's booties." It was his school and he took pride in it. And he didn't care being called a janitor instead of the next generation's title of "maintenance engineer." I know he was there in spirit with a tear in his eye when they so ruthlessly bulldozed his old building into rubble. They write books nowadays about excellence. Mr. Taylor practiced it long before I could spell it.

But we did challenge him. I still wonder how he cleaned all the glue out of my desk. Remember the old lift top desks? And how you always wondered why they had those holes in the top? It was for you to place a jar of white paste glue in upside down and play with it while Mrs. Roderick tried to teach you something about the most boring stuff in the world. I'm not sure if she realized I unscrewed the cap accidentally and the paste ran all over the inside of my desk. I do remember as clear as yesterday that whatever she tried to teach us that period, very few sitting next to me heard a word of it. They were all engrossed with me trying to be calm as I saw the paste jar turn from white to clear. My not so subtle peek inside as I casually lifted the desktop just a bit probably turned my face from red to white.

The second story windows were just right for 3rd and 4th graders. We could stand there with elbows on the window sills and philosophize as only 3rd and 4th graders can do. Remember those inventions that threw horror into the lives of kids everywhere—the achievement tests? Every spring as sure as the grass turned green, we awaited that day of torture. Inevitably we all did well. Surely a psychological plot to stress us to the limit, then assure that each of us would get sufficient strokes to satisfy us and our parents that yes, the educational system was alive and well. Those of us who thought ourselves intelligent were told that we were equivalent to a 5th grader. Those who weren't smart or were unmotivated were told that they were as smart as a 3rd grader and that's not too bad since we were 3rd graders. How can you lose? I always came out a grade or two ahead, but they never rushed out to promote me to the 5th grade. In those days, nothing resembled gifted classes or special treatment either for the smart or not so smart kids. We were all equal. It was a ploy to keep us motivated and convince us that there was hope after all. It did make our mothers feel proud and isn't that what it was all about?

Back to the windows and keeping up traditions. Only this time, it was trying to prove that the intelligence those tests said we had was real. Maybe the tests did bring out wisdom. We'd lean on the window, usually open since it was May, and look out during a break from the testing and proclaim with 9-year-old maturity, "yes sir, looking at all this green is soothing on the eyes." It was not the eyes that needed a break, though. It was the sitter and the thinker that was being clobbered. But it sure did sound smart and mature to prophesize from our lofty perch—that we could see the world and we knew all the answers.

Actually, another reason we loved the big open windows was that it gave us fresh air. And we needed it since our classmate Louis was in those closed up rooms with us. I don't remember anything else about Louis except he had either poor dietary habits or poor control over certain muscles. There were times we couldn't wait for recess so we could rush out for fresh air. Louis may have been a nice kid, but who could stand to find out. The guy probably rose to be president of a multinational corporation, assuming he learned discretion somewhere along the way.

Springtime sticks in my mind concerning the school. What else is greater than May, when the weather is warm, the world is green, and we are about to leave Mrs. Bundy's 3rd grade and go into Mrs. Roderick's 4th grade? That in itself had a basic unfairness since we had Mrs. Roderick for 2nd grade a year ago. Somewhere in those pre-teen years, someone had to teach us that the world isn't fair after all. Nothing against Mrs. Roderick, mind you; it was the principle of the thing. She had us figured out and we would not have that two month grace period with new teachers before they figure out what we are up to. Anyway, May was like holding a storm back that is ready to hit in full fury. But we had to make it till June.

Well, we had to make it until May 29th. That was my birthday. And that birthday became a tradition for eight years, thanks to my mother. Since May 29 was invariably a day or two before school ended, my mother always had a party for my birthday. Embarrassing enough by the time I reached the 8th grade, but I still lived for it. She would bring a cake and ice cream for the entire class and I'd end up posing with the teacher for a snapshot on the Kodak Brownie long before videos and even home movies. But what are high school yearbooks for if not to sneak in those snapshots of Mrs. Bundy, 3rd graders stuffing their mouths with cake and of course good ol' Joe standing on the steps of the old North Ward School with good ol' Mrs. Bundy? Those wise guys could jeer "teacher's pet" all they wanted. They loved the cake and ice cream.

Although the school was in a quiet part of town, we still were indoctrinated with safety training. We had "patrol boys" (I don't remember any "patrol girls"—after all, this was pre-feminist, conservative, downstate Illinois), who had the heavy responsibility to protect our peers from speeding autos. Nowadays, I notice the parents and grandparents protecting the street crossings, sipping coffee in SUVs and mini-vans awaiting the arrival of their kids. We were tough in our day, we protected ourselves. No wimps then. Well, naturally I jumped at the chance to be one of those guardians. Actually, I jumped at the chance to get out of class ten minutes early and the chance to wear the white belt and shoulder strap. Ron Dick was on one corner, Phil Crist on another and I was somewhere in between. I don't remember anything about shepherding kids safely across the street (the school was not exactly in a high traffic area), but I vividly remember having quick draw contests with Ron and Phil using that simplest and oldest of weapons—the finger gun. I was Roy Rogers protecting the good guys or Audie Murphy creaming the Japs. It was prestigious and I was one of the honor guards of the 4th grade: Patrol Boy. Even the words carried the power of the job. Both Ron and Phil have departed this earth, but whether or not they reached the pinnacles of success, at least we all shared the right beginnings. We protected our classmates and what more can you ask?

Such are the memories the mind protects. The old North Ward is no more nor has been for many years. I remember less and less of those years and the people in them. But there were good times that will never be again. For me of course, but for new kids as well. How can you have those same experiences in the modern schools of today that lack that basic character, as well as the Mr. Taylors, Mrs. Rodericks, Mrs. Bundys? The sterile tile hallways with rows of lookalike lockers. How can that compare with the basement of the old North Ward with its row of benches along the wall underneath the old brass coat hooks; the wooden boot puller that helped many rubber overshoes come off and go flying into the corner, to wait until springtime and exasperated mothers.

I don't remember much of what I learned about arithmetic and writing at the old North Ward. Not even how many rooms were in the building. But I'll never forget Mr. Taylor and his polished floors and his pride in caring for them and for us. The windows overlooking the grassy field and the entire world as seen from the second floor. Those magnificent stairs, from which we left each day a little wiser and older.

SIX

OLD HIGH SCHOOL– NEW NORTH WARD GRADE SCHOOL

THE LARGE BRICK building on the corner of East Sale and North Niles Streets—tucked in the residential center of Tuscola—was the old high school, dating to the early twentieth century. My dad came from his home 60 miles south to attend his senior year at this school, since his small rural school didn't graduate high school students. My mom attended this school, too; her father helped with its construction by hauling bricks from the railroad. It was a stately two-story building, full of windows. My brother attended high school through his junior year, then for his senior year attended the brand new high school in the south-east corner of town. Sort of the opposite of what our father had done nearly forty years previously.

The school and grounds took up two city blocks, bounded by Overton, Indiana, Sale and Niles Streets. The back area was the track and ball field; the outline of the track is still visible from aerial photos of nearly a century later. It had a gym and auditorium as well as two stories of classrooms. Students graduating from this school had for years become the town fathers and mothers of the town I grew up in.

In 1957, when the old North Ward was bulldozed after my fourth grade, we attended fifth grade classes in a brand new two-story annex built onto the north side of the old high school. Although physically part of the large old building, we were separated as surely as if by a huge brick wall, which in reality we were. The staid high school students that year were subjected to the screams and yells of grade-schoolers playing on what had been their sacred field. Swings and other playthings were installed so we could recreate during recess, the boys still chased the girls, the girls pretended to be offended and we used up excess energy the teachers needed a respite from.

The next year, my north-of-the-tracks class was sent south. We attended sixth grade in the South Ward School, the only time many of us attended that other stately school. At the start of my seventh grade year, the old high school became the North Ward Grade School.

We quickly claimed possession as we were now the older students in the building. I had my first male teacher—Elmer Broyles. Looking back at the May 29 birthday picture, I notice new faces, as former South Warders now joined the old crowd of the early-alphabet students north of the tracks: JoEllen Cunningham joined Glenda Cook, Rudd Callahan, Doug Carnine, and other former South Ward students, now that all our class was together for the first time.

I cannot remember much of what happened in this grand old building, nor much of what it looked like from the inside. But I do remember there were bullies back then and I was the favorite of Junior Donnals. I think his dad was a school janitor in one of the schools, but I was terrified of Junior. One cold winter day I wore my coonskin cap to school; Dad was a coon hunter and had one made into a cap. Junior grabbed onto the tail of the hat and ripped it off. I was furious but what could I do? One thing that bullied small kids can do very well is run and I did just that.

High school music teacher Carl Kohrt expanded his influence to the grade school as he started several of us on various instruments. I chose cornet since it seemed simple enough. Small to hold and just three valves. The girls chose flutes and clarinets; I didn't like the idea of a slide for the trombone or the reed for the saxophones. We had practice rooms where we played while Mr. Kohrt showed us better ways to tongue our mouthpieces or keep time. I could now read music, which I thought pretty cool. Although I could read it, I had a harder time actually playing it. We had to practice at home and have our parents sign a form saying that yes, we did practice an hour a day or whatever it was. Thankfully my dad didn't accurately time my playing, although I'm sure he would have sworn that noise lasted much longer than it did.

The next year—eighth grade—we were given a preview of what high school would soon be about. We shared some teachers and had to move to different classrooms and not sit all day in one homeroom with one teacher. Janet Southard was my homeroom teacher, but I remember Bill Burris taught us science. The big event was one day we discovered an anatomy book sitting on a table and the boys were quick to turn to the pages of naked women. We learned things some of us didn't know yet. Do I remember anything else about what I learned in eighth grade? Yes.

To graduate from eighth grade, we had to pass a test on the U.S. Constitution. It was considered so important, it was taught by Mr. Mann, the Superintendent of Schools. We gathered in the large auditorium and listened every day for a week as Mr. Mann went over all the details of what governs our country. Over sixty years later, I still have the paperback book that I studied so hard back then: *Your Rugged Constitution* by Bruce and Esther Findlay. I still refer to it.

We all passed, and we assembled in that auditorium for graduation, receiving diplomas from Mr. Mann himself. We even had a graduation dance. We were ready to move to the big time—the first class to attend the brand new high school for all four years.

There was something important to me in walking the halls and sitting in rooms that had housed both parents and my older brother. I always listened for ghosts, but my maturing interest heard nothing. In later years, I was able to contemplate the significance and continuity of such a history. How many people now can say they went to the same school building as their parents?

I want to go back and wander through the halls. I have no memory of a cafeteria, because my house was only three blocks away, and I went home for lunch. I want to sit again in the auditorium with those fixed wooden seats and look down from the balcony onto the stage. I yearn to look out the large windows onto Sale Street, to see the Methodist Church, the elms (with their painted white strips for Dutch Elm disease control) and maples lining the streets, the railroad one block south with the trains passing back and forth blaring their horns. I only have vague memories of the gym—which my father rushed from after showering and running to Miss Bertha Flack's class at the other end of the building; I don't know which classroom, but I want to stand silently and try to hear her click the lock and to hear him go slowly down to the principal to complain.

That grand old building stayed in use for the next forty years. The school board finally decided that the costs of fixing it up to meet standards were not worth it when compared to its age and the cost of a new building. Its days were numbered, repeating the history of the old North Ward and the South Ward. A new South Ward grade school had been built across the street from the new high school to replace the old South Ward. Now the voters finally decided to fund a new school (north of N. Line Street), to replace the historic North Ward building. It had served four generations, but now a new building awaited. Finally, it was demolished to make a very large vacant lot. I have a brick from that building, as well as one from the South Ward, that sit on my desk in a place of honor. Bricks will last forever, much longer than the fading memory of an aging schoolboy. I smile as I think of the generations of students who walked those halls, sat in the classrooms, and looked out the windows and wondered about the world.

I attended three brick buildings for grades one through eight. None now exist. The old high school-new North Ward was the last to be bulldozed. When they tear down your childhood schools, something more than a building is lost. Only memories are now left.

SEVEN

THE SOUTH WARD GRADE SCHOOL

I<small>T IS A</small> gray, cold and windy November day. The kind that seems to reduce one to a mournful longing for just about anything else at any other time: a warm sunny September sky; flowers of a July Rocky Mountain afternoon; birds welcoming an April morning; or, even the melancholy ache for long-ago times right here.

It is that time I think of now: October 1959 with the Dodgers (or Yankees—they seemed to meld into one another in those years) in the World Series. I was in the 6th grade—Mrs. McDaniel's class—sitting in our room on the multi-windowed second floor of the South Ward Grade School. Someone brought in a TV and we watched the World Series during class.

All World Series games were day games, and the world seemed to stop on those October afternoons. It was a ritual—an important national event. Nothing equals it today. Not the hype of a commercial Super Bowl, not the panoply of New Year's bowl games, not even the sordid fascination of celebrity trials or impeachment hearings. It was a ritual that defined mid-century middle America and is gone as surely as the old South Ward.

And that is my dirge on this gray November day. The old South Ward is gone, along with the meaning of such things as the World Series where players played for team and honor, not multimillion-dollar salaries. I stand here not on a sunny exciting October day in 1959, but a memory-filled cloudy day in 1994. And I see not that great brick building, but instead construction crews building houses and apartments on these acres of history. The magnificent brick edifice was torn down years ago. Gone, like the old North Ward before it.

Bounded by Niles, Daggy, Ohio and Wilson Streets, the South Ward was torn down and the expanse was vacant for how many years? That stately old white pine stands like a tombstone guarding the grave of memories of brick and glass, and the fading echoes of screaming kids. Nothing else remained save the acres of grass. Nothing was deserving as a successor to this stately old building. Nothing like the houses that were sacrilegiously—to me—planted on the grounds of the old North Ward, erasing any memory of that historic building and schoolyard.

Until today. I watch construction workers moving like misty ghosts in time, throughout the nearly-completed homes and condominiums, destroying my memories, and creating memories for people I don't know and never will. They will live their lives not knowing the spirits of this field.

My grandfather Hance may have hauled bricks from the railroad cars on the nearby tracks for the South Ward school, as he did for the old high school north of the tracks. Bricks that soon joined together to form a building that symbolized the pride and hope of a community. Bricks that formed the walls that sheltered thousands of youth over how many generations. Youth who have grown up, built this community and dozens of others like it, raised their own children, and have even passed the bounds of this existence. And bricks that were eventually to be unceremoniously dumped somewhere as landfill, to disappear forever into the soil from which they came.

The old Union School, the pride of the new and growing community, stood here before the South Ward. Who mourns for the memories of that building? Who even remembers it? It ushered in a new century; it watched as automobiles slowly replaced horses. It listened as children in that turn-of-the-century building recited the Gettysburg Address, discussed the building of the Panama Canal, and celebrated the end of the "war to end all wars."

Then, the fateful day. During lunch hour, a fire started and soon the building was rubble. And Mr. Roy Bird, a mail carrier, died in an attempt to go back to get something of his daughter's. A white pine was planted as his memorial. And now it is memorial to the building that sprang from the ashes. And as they cleared the debris out of the old Union School, they buried what remained, including the old chemistry lab.

And before the Union School? I could research the historical records, but that's more than I want to do now. It would go back to the Civil War, the pioneer settlers, the Illini, Kickapoo, Shawnee, Fox, or whoever lived here 500 years ago.

Other than that one year of 6th grade, I cannot personally relate much to the South Ward building. I remember going there on weekends and summers, something I have no recollection of doing at the old North Ward, which was just as close to my house, only the other direction. I grew up on the north side of the tracks, so my history was North Ward. It was like being a Cubs fan instead of a White Sox fan; you knew the National League intimately, and only knew of the vague existence of the American League. I only knew of the vague existence of the south side kids my own age. Then that stroke of fate that declared: in 1959 all 6th graders go to the South Ward.

Both the old North Ward and the South Ward had big open fields, swings and jungle gyms. But the South Ward building itself—now that was something you could get your feet onto! Unlike the old North Ward, this building had ground floor windows with ledges. I became quite skillful at traversing much of the length of the building on the window ledges, about 3 or 4 feet above the ground. Concrete ledges wide enough for a twelve-year-old foot and if my memory serves, I may have reached that world-class master level of going the entire length of the building without falling—a feat that took months of practice and unfailing courage. Then again, maybe no one else cared and I was the only one with nothing better to do. But what is more important to a sixth grader than to challenge a great unknown and discover bounds and limits—and ledges?

Maybe I had lots of practice climbing and clinging to heights since I do remember many times I tried to climb onto the upstairs railing of the lumber yard across the street and next to the railroad tracks. It took a jump up to grab the catwalk, then hoist myself up. It took catlike skills, which I struggled to achieve. This challenge so close to the school grounds was overwhelming. Much more than the jungle gym in the schoolyard.

My most vivid memory is the legend of Mr. Cook, burned into my memory the fateful day shared with Mike Carroll and Jim Bailey. Sixth grade is the time in the flowering of youth when boys turn inexplicably insane and girls even worse—only in that coy, mysterious kind of way that entices the boys. Also when boys learn four-letter words and even what they mean. It's called hormones.

Mike, Jim, and I were at the South Ward—who knows why. It wasn't ledge climbing. Mike had a crush on Glenda. We were outside Glenda's house, almost next door to the school. Mike and Jim were shouting things at Glenda's house—things that if heard by adult ears would surprise, shock, disgust, things that to 6th-grade ears hint of adult passions, maturity and "coolness." In other words, blatant obscenity. Anyway, it backfired—Mr. Cook happened to be home and happened to hear us and happened to deal with this situation and not ignore it.

Mike, Jim, and I ended up on the roof of a small addition to the school building trying to escape a rather furious father. What we had seen as humor was not humorous to him. We botched our escape, and trapped on the roof, had to endure a lecture by Mr. Cook. Not a gentle father-son type of lecture. Mr. Cook did have a son; he also had two daughters. That must change a man's perspective. The lecture quite vividly evoked scenes of bodily harm and a short, lonely life if we ever tried something like we were mouthing off.

The scene must have been classic. Three twelve-year-olds running madly behind houses, scrambling around the complex of buildings and annexes of the huge brick building, panic-stricken as we searched for a hiding place, laughing about our escape. Then, hearing the voice of one mad adult. Like cornered rats, trapped, huddled onto this little roof, looking down at this huge angry man looking up at us with fire in his eyes. The thoughts running through our minds evoked sheer terror; we could be expelled, tortured, sent off to reform school. Our parents would kill us. Or worse. Top scholars, future athletes, all future possibilities flashed in ruin before our eyes.

Needless to say, this event is etched in my memory of the South Ward. And of Mr. Cook and Glenda and Mike and four-letter words. It couldn't have been too bad, though. Mike dated Glenda a few years later. I was too shy to ever speak to her but I worked with both Mr. and Mrs. Cook while employed at the Four Seasons Department Store during high school. They never said a word to me about the episode. I can visualize Mr. Cook chuckling about the whole affair later. Well, it worked for me—he scared the bejeebers out of me. I don't know about Mike and Jim, but I was glad to let the whole thing just fade into oblivion. Years later, Mike had small plaques made for Jim and me engraved with: "I could have sent you to reform school. Bill Cook." I still chuckle about that.

The scene of that episode is no more. I have no idea where Glenda is, but I certainly know where Mike is. I go back with Mike about as far as anyone and I share a bond with him that will never disappear. Best childhood friends don't always stay in touch over the years and miles, but we were close in those early years. Even such episodes as Mike throwing rocks at me as I walked home from school one day are overshadowed by scenes of us throwing a frisbee at each other in a blinding snowstorm at night during a college Christmas break. And a trip to Philadelphia with his minister and the scene of the minister being pulled over for speeding and saying "God as my witness, I wasn't speeding. Was I boys?" And long discussions on politics and philosophy and those things that bond till death do you part.

But I can't help but throw mental rocks at Mike now. How dare you be the one to finally fill in that open grave of the South Ward? Better you, though, than anyone else. I know you share these same feelings of history and youth and the importance of ghosts of brick and glass. You see, Michael, those are ghosts and spirits that are haunting you now. The spirits of the South Ward and even the remains of the old Union School that frustrated your efforts to dig for a waterline; the soil bursting into flame as your contractor unearthed the old chemistry bottles buried during its long-ago demolition. Dirt doesn't burn, but spirits do. Be kind to them, Mike, and tell the new owners of these houses to respect them. On a quiet October afternoon, have them turn off their TVs and radios and listen. Listen to the echoes of a class of 6th graders cheering on the Yankees or the Dodgers as Mickey Mantle or Duke Snyder steps to the plate.

Mike, you cannot feel what I feel here. You decided to stay and age with the town. I didn't. Whenever I return, I return to the town and life that froze in time. The town called Tuscola that ended for me in 1965. I return to 1965 every time I re-enter Tuscola. In a way, this is a wonderful ability. It's something you cannot do and it gives me a window for time travel. But it is also sad for it vividly reminds me of something lost and gone forever.

The South Ward is one of the memories that was shattered while I was gone. It disappeared, but I could still come back and stand on that wide field, guarded by a tall white pine and see the building. It's there, just invisible to most. But now, it is fading fast—even to me. The field has disappeared as homes now invade it. The ghosts have been forced to leave. But ghosts do have a way of staying on; they reside now in my mind. And just maybe, on an October afternoon, they will return. But you have to look carefully and listen. It helps to close your eyes. I hear it now—the bell, the scuffle to the chairs. The drawing of my attention to the bright sunshine flowing through those many windows. The big pine tree that makes me think of the wide-open West I am starting to long for. Mrs. McDaniel says we are to learn how to divide and multiply fractions this week. And our scrapbook on some country in South America is due in three weeks. And a spelling test tomorrow. Oh, how I wish I could be grown up and not have to learn all this stuff. Time just seems to go so slowly. What is Mike doing over there? Is he passing a note to Glenda? A train whistles and passes by, clicking and clacking on the tracks. How much time is left until school is out?

EIGHT

Tuscola Community High School

SCHOOLS DEFINE A community. To adults, the quality of schools ensures the future of the community and the pride and success they reflect of the citizens themselves. To the kids, they are simply a place where you grow up and create memories. You spend a lot of time there and you get to know the buildings like the adults never do. I was never that concerned about the quality of the education I was getting. I was concerned about the teachers and their personality quirks, and the ease of getting good grades from them. In retrospect, I'm glad someone else was looking after me, for my appreciation of schools and teachers left something to be desired.

Over the years, I have felt dismayed, saddened, and greatly disappointed that the school district chose to bulldoze three of my childhood schools: the old North Ward, the new North Ward (old high school), and South Ward. The new high school is the only one left standing of the schools I attended. It was relatively new when I started my intimate discovery of it in 1962—the pride of Tuscola. It is next to the cemetery, on the southeast edge of town, where the growth and future of Tuscola was to be. The downtown was dying and the old schools that graced the center of town disappeared. This was the 1960s and the sprawl of growth was in the developments east and south of downtown. The new high school is conveniently located to look past the history of the town—in the form of the

48

cemetery—and face the future, along Route 36. I was part of that future, along with several hundred others who attended Tuscola Community Unit High School; I never understood the verbiage for the school name, but the town elders must have good reasons. We were the Warriors—the Old Gold and Black—and I was part of the class of '65, the Greatest Class Alive, ninety-nine members strong.

The seniors during my freshman year were the first class to spend all four years in that building. My brother's class of '59 was the first class to graduate from it. It was still new enough we could consider it our own, not part of the long history of the town, its elders, and the story of Tuscola. All that memory stuff lay in the old high school—the new North Ward Grade School—where I attended 7th and 8th grades.

I am part of the generation called the *baby boomers*: we were to lead the nation into the prosperity of the twentieth century. But all it meant to me was a new building—mostly all on one floor—with long hallways, lockers that weren't trashed yet, a big gym and lots of parking. And a long way from anywhere else in town.

When the class of '65 entered that building in September 1962, there were no Beatles, John Kennedy was president, the Mustang was still dormant in Lee Iacocca's vision, the Strand Theater still showed first-run movies, and Gus still dominated downtown with his phosphates and hamburgers. There was a McDonalds in Champaign, but it didn't show how many billions it had sold yet. The University of Illinois Assembly Hall was under construction and people thought the roof would collapse. There was no Interstate, and color TV was still a luxury of the rich. But life was good for most 14-year-olds and we started making memories in the long hallways of the high school. We didn't know it but our generation was on the cusp of changing the world, at least according to us a few years later.

I was small and shy. I don't think the word "nerd" was in existence then, but I was one. I was a loner, didn't socialize much, and spent my time and energy getting good grades. I didn't mingle with anyone older than me. Seniors were in a different world, and juniors and sophomores were just wanna be seniors. The whole concept of not having homeroom and roving from class to class was new. We were introduced to the idea in 8th grade, sharing a few teachers, but we still were mostly in one teacher's class. This shuffle from class to class was scary at first. It made me feel rather homeless and a little insecure. What if I forgot which class was next? And moving down hallways with students three years older than me? That heightened my insecurity. I was intimidated by the older students and had no friends or even acquaintances with people older than me. It took me until I was a sophomore and junior to feel even slightly comfortable with them. Of course, when I became an upperclassman myself, I did nothing to make the younger classes comfortable.

The rows of metal lockers did a lot to separate the classes. I have no memory of where each class was located. It shifted year to year, but the hallway for our class served as the makeshift homeroom. We gathered there in the morning and between classes. That small locker became my security blanket and I knew of no one who kept anything even remotely illegal or immoral in their lockers. It simply was an anchor.

After I graduated, I only set foot in the building one time over the next fifty years, as I attended a basketball game on one of my annual trips home to visit the folks. I have tried to remember the layout of the building but mainly remember the long halls. As you entered from the front of the building, which few people did, the main office was the first thing you saw. Then the cases with all the sports trophies. Straight through the big double doors was the gym. Turn right down the long hall were the classrooms and labs for science—chemistry, physics, and biology. Past that were the home-ec rooms, including kitchens. On the other side of the hall were the large rooms for agriculture and industrial arts. I spent many hours in the science rooms, but never set foot in the home-ec, ag and shop areas.

There were no boys in the home-ec classes, nor were there any girls in the ag or shop classes. This was a loss for both and hopefully, nowadays things are different, although, in most schools, home-ec is no longer taught. I always felt boys should have been required to attend home-ec since there were many skills taught there that I and most males could have benefitted from. In this liberated age, maybe someone thought home-ec was sexist or not politically correct. I consider those subjects to be life skills but then sometimes I have wondered what has happened to those skills I considered to be common sense. Maybe there should have been classes called "common sense skills."

South of the main office were the wings—two stories, with a library and adjacent study hall. English, history, math, and social studies were on the first floor, with business classes upstairs. There was no elevator, but to my knowledge, we never had a student who couldn't climb stairs.

When I took typing as a freshman, the typewriter was the only useful tool this skill applied to. I knew I would be writing a lot, so typing was a no-brainer. Today, I imagine keyboarding—which it is now called—is learned in kindergarten. I don't use a smartphone, so a computer keyboard is the only use I make and it certainly is much easier than on my old manual Smith-Corona, which is gathering dust in my root cellar.

As I started high school, some of the teachers were institutions. Harriet Sluss taught Latin, Dorothy Deer biology, Alberta Magnussen typing. They were ancient in my eyes. I know Miss Deer had taught my father and I knew for certain Miss Sluss must have taught Abraham Lincoln. Latin—who spoke Latin? Spanish was the only other choice, although I have benefitted from knowing Latin all my adult life. Many English words came from Latin and of course, being a biologist, I found Latin very beneficial in understanding scientific names. I would probably have been better served to take Spanish, but that was taught by Miss Sluss as well. French was added later.

Other teachers included the feared Bill Butkovich for boys PE, and Miriam Cox for girls. I guess you had to be an athlete to appreciate Bukko, as we called him. I once interviewed him for a sports article since I was the sports editor for the weekly *Tuscola Journal*. I had written questions on a note pad I referred to as I talked to him. He tried to watch what I was writing, which made me nervous for a couple of reasons. I had never tried to write standing up holding a notebook. Plus, as a nervous freshman with low self-confidence interviewing a fearsome coach and former University of Illinois football player, I was very uncomfortable. I had Gene Murray for PE rather than Bukko, but Gene, the nice guy he may have been, also intimidated me.

As the sports editor for the *Tuscola Journal*, I was also the cub reporter. I ran up and down the sidelines at football games taking notes and keeping statistics. I was obvious—not for my size, which was small— but the fact I wore the uniform of the Tuscola Warriors marching band. A few minutes before the end of the first half I had to run into the building to get my cornet and be prepared to come marching out in formation. We did not do the precision formations they do nowadays; each game had a theme and we formed pictures and outlines of things related to what we were playing. Once we marched off the field, I ran inside, put away my cornet, raced out with my clipboard, and quickly asked people what happened during the few minutes I missed at the end of the first half.

This was home games. I don't remember going to away games, and for those I had to make up my article by reading the box score in the daily Champaign paper. Needless to say, those articles were not my best. During my junior year, I was the official statistician for the basketball team so attended the away games on the team bus. They didn't invite me back my senior year. I think I didn't fit in with the jocks. I quit my sports editor job my senior year and eased out of paying attention to sports.

I enjoyed mathematics, especially geometry, but struggled with quadratic equations and algebra. The Lionbergers were the math teachers, Warren and Dorothy. My favorite subject was biology with Miss Deer. We dissected frogs and starfish and talked about human sexuality. I remember one day Miss Deer had Glenda Cook read part of the text that dealt with human sexual reproduction and all of us were squirming in our seats, none more than Glenda. That was the closest we came to sex education, but we must have somehow been paying attention because I didn't know of any girl who became pregnant in high school. I expect luck had something to do with that because birth control pills were only then becoming available.

The annual field trip to Turkey Run State Park in Indiana was a highlight of our sophomore spring term. That was when I first realized there was such a thing as a wildflower. I thought the term exciting: a flower that was wild. Imagine that. The ensuing project of collecting tree leaves shaped the remainder of my life. I have always thanked Miss Deer for that life-changing influence.

In our junior year, our English teacher, Mrs. Rager, had transferred from California. She was relatively young, quite attractive, and had the attention of all the boys in our class. One time I tried to impress her before class started by sharing my recent reading of some of Socrates's works. But I blew it when I said I was reading some of Pluto's works; Bob Nunn not so politely corrected me when he said "Pluto was the dog, Plato was the writer." I didn't try to impress Mrs. Rager again.

Bob was my table mate in our senior study hall, and was probably the smartest one in our entire class of '65. I will never forget one October day in 1964. Bob, Tom McDaniel, and one other classmate and I went to Champaign to hear Barry Goldwater give a campaign speech. That night, Bob shot himself in the head. To this day, we still debate whether it was accidental or suicide. We will never know. I found out about his death the next morning when I went to work at the Tastee Freeze. I told Nancy Norton as she came to work. Her comment was "you are kidding." Of course, I wasn't and it was a shock to the whole class. He was there one day and forever gone the next.

Later that fall of senior year, I was given a new table partner in study hall. Martha Smith was a popular girl. She was very outgoing and was later voted Most Unpredictable in the 1965 TCHS Yearbook. I didn't know Martha very well, but we hit it off. We started flirting, not in any romantic way, but just to be, well, unpredictable. We would rub knees under the table, write each other notes, kid about eloping or running off together. I would have been scared to death to go on a date with her and she probably wouldn't have been caught dead doing such a thing, but we had fun joking about it. Butkovich, who was the monitor of the study hall was constantly coming over to shush us. We never took the hint and continued our fun times. Finally, he came over and almost picked me up and moved me to another table on the far side of the room. It was all over and we didn't see each other much after that. My mother would have been horrified if she read what Martha wrote in my yearbook "I hope you have given up your plans to run off and get married." Decades later, I found the notebook Martha and I passed back and forth writing notes to each other; it was especially heartbreaking since about that time I heard about Martha's death. She had been one of the few classmates to visit me in April 2002 when I returned to clean out the house after my father passed. She and I sat on the front steps and just talked. We never went back to those silly study hall days, but she knew my visit was stressful for me and she was willing to share a few minutes of her life. I will always think highly of her for that.

There were usually dances in the cafeteria after football and basketball games. The cafeteria served as the place to eat lunches but also the auditorium for plays and other events. I often went home for lunch, but would occasionally eat there. I vividly remember one day sitting at a table with Chud Corey, the janitor. He was an institution and like Mr. Taylor in the old North Ward, he took pride in his work of keeping the school in good and clean shape. We were eating fried chicken and I noticed Chud choking. He couldn't breathe and was starting to slump over. We students looked at each other and didn't know what to do—this was before the Heimlech Manuver was invented. Either someone slapped his back or else he finally got the chicken past his windpipe. He was thoroughly embarrassed, as were we as we watched him in total helplessness.

In my senior year, for some reason I decided to run for class vice president. I have no idea who I ran against, but I won. Doug Carnine was president and I don't remember ever doing one single thing as VP. I was informed years later that Doug deferred to me to decide actions in response to Bob Nunn's death. It was close to Homecoming and the Senior Class questioned whether it was proper to do a senior float. Doug knew I was a close friend of Bob and said I should decide for the class. I must have said yes, but much that happened in that tumultuous month of October 1964 blurs in my memory. All within a few weeks, my favorite St. Louis Cardinals won the World Series, Khrushchev was deposed in the Soviet Union, Viet Nam was starting to dominate the news, and Bob tragically died. The Beatles burst on the scene soon after.

We all looked for things to do that would be listed by our picture in the Yearbook. Was that why I ran for Vice President? I doubt it, but it was something to do. I was also the co-editor with Carol Schrodt of the student newspaper, *Old Gold and Black Echoes*, but again, I can't remember helping put together the editions of the paper. I did write an article or two. Miss Hall was our sponsor and she was not my favorite teacher.

I have two main memories of young, and fresh out of college, Miss Carolyn Hall, or Stick, as we ungraciously called the senior English teacher behind her back. One memory is that she said the correct way to pronounce the name of the Roman Cicero was "Kicker Oh," not "Siss er Oh." And Don Juan was not "Wan" but "Jew awn." The other memory is when she called me after class to ask if I was considering suicide. She didn't put it that way, but she was concerned about a poem I wrote as an assignment. My character was a medieval knight who went off to battle expecting to die. I said no, it was just something that came to mind. I give her credit for being alert decades before that became a genuine concern for teenagers. She surprised me during the senior awards right before graduation when she awarded me the Senior English award. I was stunned and have forever since then wanted to contact her and apologize for the unkind thoughts I had towards her. She faded into the mists, but I hope our ungrateful class did not discourage her from teaching. Miss Hall, wherever you are, I apologize.

She did give our senior English class a memorable moment when one day she didn't come to class because of a last-minute illness. We all sat there for a few minutes after the bell rang, then when we realized we had no teacher, we had chair races around the room. It was a ball until the principal showed up and sent us to study hall.

Another memorable time was in Ethel Snider's social science class, or Fat Ethel as we referred to her, as only adolescents can cruelly do. We didn't respect her, so while she was talking, John Edmiston or Allen Michener or some other miscreant would call out "f..k." We called it a "f..k calling" contest. She never caught on. She would look around and ask if someone had a question. We would snicker and giggle, look angelic, then do it again. Do I remember anything else from that class? Of course not.

We had a guidance counselor, Bruce Knicely, but I don't remember talking to him. What he was guiding was unknown to me. Maybe he only counseled troubled students or failing ones. Maybe I knew what I wanted to do and where to go to college and thus was left alone. I hope he helped some. Donna

Ard told me years later that his guidance to her was not to waste her parents' money going to college; she should marry well. I was shocked if that was the type of guidance he gave. I have no doubt some of my classmates didn't know what they wanted or where to go after graduating. Some never did. Maybe I was lucky.

A tradition that we took advantage of was Senior Skip Day. Near graduation, the seniors headed for the four winds on the last day of carefree adventure while the lesser undergrads had to attend class. I originally was going over to Indiana with Roy Davis and Rudd Callahan and go swimming in some old water-filled mining pits. After careful consideration and the thought that this was how teenage boys drowned, I canceled out. I instead invited myself to go with Mike Carroll and Tom McDaniel to St. Louis. They wanted to go golfing, then attend a St. Louis Cardinal baseball game. I could care less about golf, but I served as a caddy. We stayed at the Y after we attended the ball game. When we stopped by the stadium in the afternoon to get tickets for the night game, the ticket seller told us, with a rather straight face, the game was canceled. As we started to complain, he laughed and said it was because of a flood in the outfield; he was referring to star player Curt Flood. Later at the game, as we had seats at the edge of the upstairs tier, Tom leaned over the edge and dropped a cigarette he had been smoking. It landed on a man far below who let out a yelp, then looked up. We had discretely disappeared up the aisles for a few minutes. I don't remember who won the game.

Our cohort of nearly 100 had spent much of the previous eight years together in grade school, changing school buildings, and greeting new classmates as they moved to town or saying goodbye to others as they moved on. I considered all that to be growing up. We played, we learned, we grew together and at times apart. But when we entered high school, something changed. All of a sudden, we realized we were still growing up, but now we were maturing. Not that many of us did a good job of the latter, but we were getting there. By our senior year, things got serious as we all realized we soon needed to go out into the world on our own and be somebody, not just a student anymore. As I write this over fifty years later, I think back and see how most of us turned out. We have lost over ten of our classmates and I have been shocked to learn who they were. For aging baby boomers, we have stayed on this earth, but we scattered to the winds and no longer know each other very well if at all. But those four years of high school, preceded by the eight of grade school, gave us memories we've kept for a lifetime.

NINE

THE STRAND THEATER

THE STRAND THEATER. Say those three words to anyone from mid-century Tuscola and it brings a smile and a rush of memories. Eaten by flames on a cold December night in 1967, the Strand still appears like an apparition in the minds of Boomers and older Tuscolians, as we reminisce of our youth.

It was downtown, on the south side of Sale Street, across from the Ben Franklin, North's Furniture, Nick's, and the pool hall; between Young's Electric and the Montgomery Ward Catalog Store; and two doors down from the *Tuscola Review*. The Tuscola National Bank still occupied the northwest corner at Sale and Main, the grand old Hotel Douglas on the northeast corner, and Gus's on the southwest.

Saturday afternoon matinees were often double features. The bicycles would pile up on the sidewalk and we would line up to pay our money. I don't remember any bicycle racks. No one thought of chains or padlocks; who could imagine anyone stealing a bike? We could ride all over town by ourselves, exploring our own worlds. But pedestrians and car drivers knew to avoid Sale Street at movie let-out time. Bikes careened off the curb, into the street, and headed all over town—bad guys from the movie might have been chasing the riders, or we might have been fleeing from the Blob.

My former classmates have had disagreements over the admission price. Some say it was a quarter, some fifteen cents, I even thought a dime. (I may have mixed that up with the cost of a comic book.) Whatever the admission to the Strand, we gladly paid it to disappear for an hour or two in a fantasy world brought to life on a Saturday afternoon or Friday night.

The Strand Theater embodied the small town enchantment of a Tuscola that no longer exists. But it does exist, in our minds. We may struggle to recollect the details. But the stories that big screen brought to life for ten-year-old imaginations were priceless. The world opened up to us and we were up to the task. The cowboys and gunslingers of the old west may have been fictitious, but they gave us heroes. There may not have been giant mantises or *Godzillas* or *The Blob*, but Hollywood gave us worlds to imagine, to have nightmares or wishful dreams, of *Cinderellas* or *Snow Whites*. Fantasies could come true like John Wayne winning over Capucine in *North to Alaska*. I saw that movie three times. I'm pretty sure it was the scene of Capucine in the bathtub. As I said, it was all about imaginations.

I was ten in 1957, my imagination susceptible to the wide-open spaces of the old west, the far distant galaxies of outer space, and Tarzan-filled jungles. We all watched the heroes defeat the villains, the scientists save us from the Blob or other aliens, and the brave GIs blast the enemies. Our heroes were good and wholesome and you never saw Roy saying a bad word or getting involved with some scantily clad young temptress. He just saddled up Trigger, looked lovingly at Dale, and rode off to save the world from the villains. It was a simpler world back then—the special effects were in our heads, and good versus bad was easy to figure out.

Our Saturday afternoons were predictable. Carol and Mary walked halfway across town on Saturdays to see the Westerns, quarters clutched in their hands, looking forward to Roy Rogers or Alan Ladd doing what they did best. Anne recalled her first year in Tuscola in 1957; welcomed into Mrs. Roderick's fourth grade at the old North Ward school, she remembers going to the Strand and spending her quarter.

And Bob Rogers recalled that "On Saturdays, we would get a quarter to go to the movies. 15¢ for a double feature, newsreel or two, previews, the next installment of a serial, and cartoons. Besides Smiley [Burnett], we saw Gene Autry, Roy Rogers & Dale Evans, Lash Larue, The Cisco kid and his sidekick Pancho, Rocky Lane, and all the rest. We all learned a lot about truth, honor, and what being a true friend was from our onscreen heroes."

There were award-winning movies as well. The *Wizard of Oz* held our attention like glue, but Carol remembers later being frightened of a witch at her sister Connie's 8th birthday party. She also whistled jauntily with Barb as they walked home along the railroad tracks after watching *Bridge on the River Kwai*. That movie opened up new worlds to us: a jungle and river in a place half a globe away; and war stories we later used to play GI with toy figures in the sand pile.

The *Music Man*, starring Robert Preston and Shirley Jones, was welcomed by the Tuscola High School Marching Band—led by director Carl Kohrt—playing "76 Trombones." We marched right into the theater to watch the movie. At other times, we sat mesmerized by the *Deadly Mantis* and the *Blob*, but shed tears over *Old Yeller*. We were fascinated by Elvis in *Jailhouse Rock*, although Carol says she and Allen walked out on a later Elvis movie. Elvis was the rage that our parents didn't understand; they found the likes of *An Affair to Remember* more to their tastes.

I recall the movie *Raintree County* with Elizabeth Taylor. It was a complicated movie, striving to be a new *Gone With the Wind*. I loved the theme song and of course, Taylor was a soothing sight to young eyes. When I got home from the movie, I discovered tremendous turmoil as my parents' church had fired Pastor Brandon, and the church essentially split apart. Afterwards, we went to the Congregational Church. None of that mattered to me, but *Raintree County* always will bring back this eventful time in my parents' life.

Movie headliners also included Brando, Wayne, Hepburn, Carol Baker and Cary Grant, Gable and Marilyn Monroe, Jimmy Stewart and Gary Cooper, Debbie Reynolds and Maureen

O'Hara. *Peyton Place* won awards, but to a ten-year-old, was a little too adult. I had a habit of submerging into my seat as the romantic scenes became too intense, although they would not hold a candle to some scenes of today. Times and mores change.

The Strand was to us a grand place, with the balcony for older high school types who enjoyed each other more than whatever was on the screen. And the soundproof cry-room enabled young parents to go to the movies with their young children, some of whom had probably been us a few years earlier. My mother recounted that my first movie was *Bambi* in 1948.

The Strand was built in the late teens. Silents were the only choice then, but not even my parents would remember Frieda Rhodes playing the piano and cueing the movies until George Barber bought the theater in 1929. By 1930, he had remodeled it so talkies could be played. I remember a much older Ted Cox as the pianist at the Presbyterian Church, but he arrived in 1939 to play at the Strand. A real orchestra used the orchestra pit on Sundays and accompanied such famous names as Hoot Gibson and Smiley Burnette.

Much of this was before my time, but for me, the Strand was always there, until that fateful night in 1967. I was home for Christmas from college, and on Christmas eve, I heard sirens and saw the glowing orange sky two blocks from my house. I ran outside, saw the commotion, grabbed my coat, and ran downtown. The Strand was engulfed in flames, and a crowd was gathering. Fire trucks were shooting streams of water, police were telling us to stay away. Heroes emerged that night. Denny Dietrich and his volunteer firefighters fought valiantly to save the rest of downtown. Amos Albritton courageously made his way into the alley to shut off the gas. Someone from the power company turned off the electricity. We huddled in fear and in awe of the spectacle. I visited with old friends, we told stories, watched as some people choked back tears, and worried over other buildings. We all knew the inevitable result.

Tuscola would never be the same. It was determined that the fire started at the Montgomery Ward store next door. The theater would never be rebuilt. Downtown was doomed as downtowns all across the country were dying. Life went to the edges, the strip malls. Life slowly died along Sale Street after the ash cooled. Many small towns had their Strands, most to fall victim to newer theaters or even theater complexes on the edges of town. Those new theaters could never come close to the atmosphere, the class of the Strand.

TEN

GUS'S

LOCATED ON THE southwest corner of Sale and Main Streets, Gus's was at the hub of downtown. It had been there for years by the time I knew it. I have seen old black and white pictures of Gus as a young man—or at least middle-aged—probably taken in the '30s. Gus was an institution, as was his business. I cannot remember its actual business name. Was it the Candy Kitchen? Was it a restaurant, or a soda fountain, or a candy store? We just called it Gus's.

I didn't eat there often, but I do remember a few hamburgers I ate on special occasions. Mostly I remember the phosphates; my favorite was the suicide, which included every flavor in his row of syrups.

To my thirteen-year-old eyes, the marble counter seemed huge. Old-fashioned stools lined its length, with a full-length mirror on the wall behind the counter. The sculpted metal ceiling was common for these old buildings; I always wondered how they made such a thing. It was a work of art that has disappeared in this modern era. Gus's was not modern, it was a landmark.

Wooden booths lined the room. There were no windows on the east (Main Street) side, so the booths had privacy. They disappeared into the dark recesses where patrons ate, sipped drinks, or shared the latest in town gossip. Their world was not yet mine; my few visits were centered along the counter where I could watch the world come and go.

The experts tell us that certain smells awaken memory cells

in the brain. I cannot remember any recent hamburger smells that awaken the Gus hamburgers, but if I do smell anything similar, I know I will time travel back to those days. Did he have fries as well? I need that memory smell to answer that question. Maybe a suicide phosphate will work, but who in the last fifty years has heard of a phosphate?

Gus was famous for his chocolates, but my teenage finances did not allow such a treat. Made in Gus's magic downstairs chocolate shop, they were there for my dreamtime.

In his broken English, Gus the Greek would ask me questions I could not understand. To him, I was just another passing generation, but he cared for me as he cared for thousands of others who had come and gone.

After I left home, in 1965, I remember Mom telling me how she would go over to Gus's on her breaks when she worked at Carpenter's at the northeast corner of Main and E.N. Central, sit in a booth and talk religion with Gus. She knew her Bible and I have no doubt Gus knew his. Their talks would have been insightful, probably filled with arguments about accuracy of the New or Old Testament. I would give anything to have been a fly on the wall for those discussions.

After sitting vacant for many years, Gus's was brought back to life by granddaughters as they restarted what Gus left years before. They recreated the institution and have awakened the love, the care, and the memories—maybe the hamburgers as well. I was sent a gift package of chocolates by classmate Bill Carson several years ago, and they filled in a gap I missed decades ago.

Gus made not only hamburgers and phosphates, chocolates and milkshakes, but memories. Oh, how he made the memories that have lasted for more than half a century for me, longer for others. I didn't realize it then, but I should have known that when Gus departed this life, no one would replace him. No one could. You cannot replace the past. It only fades into pleasant memories so full of cobwebs. Facts may end up a little distorted, maybe a little incorrect. But details fade as meanings grow.

I miss the sizzling of the hamburgers, the bite of the phosphate, the creaminess of the strawberry milkshake. I miss Gus's snarl as he pretended to be gruff and stern; it was a snarl of love that he made with tenderness. His life was already history at the time I knew him. My generation was the future and Gus was the past. He was part of what made Tuscola my hometown and my childhood. As I struggle to relive a part of me, I look past the mirrors above the fountain. I look up at the sculpted ceiling, then back down as I hear a sound. I see Gus standing behind the counter wiping his hands on his apron, smiling. If Gus would turn around, what would he see in the mirror?

ELEVEN

NOTABLE TUSCOLIANS

THERE ARE LITERALLY hundreds of people I could mention here. I have selected a few that I briefly mentioned in other chapters. This is not intended to be a full description, but a brief glimpse of characters that made an impression on my early life.

❧

Doc Boylson was a town legend, bow-legged, white-haired, and bug-eyed with his glasses. He continually whistled while he inspected me, never stopping as he effortlessly filled his hypodermic needle to give me my complement of childhood shots. In those days, he would make house calls, coming on short panicky notice carrying his leather medical bag. We lost something very valuable as we progressed in medicine to the point where doctors ceased house calls. I suppose the doctors praised this as real progress, but that personal touch was a blessing that can never be forgotten.

The town doctors divided the town into factions—not intentionally, but geographically. We were the patients of Dr. Boylson, who brought me into the world. His rival was Dr. Deaver, whom I knew nothing about, other than he was a legend as well. (The town went into shock in 1965 when both he and his father-in law were killed in a car wreck on a blind intersection in the farm country outside of town.) Dr. Steiner had an office downtown but I knew nothing about him. Dr. Cunningham was another popular doc, and I knew nothing of him either, other than he had a passel of children, one of whom, JoEllen, was in my class until he transferred her to a Catholic school in Springfield. Mike Carroll, my best buddy in those days, always claimed that move was because he dated her and her dad thought Mike a rather seedy influence.

⤳

Small town politics was outside my young purview, although I do remember George Nichols, a lawyer, who most likely decided what Republican would run the town and the county. One day, I got a call that pulled me out of Janet Southard's eighth-grade class. Never having had a phone call at school, I feared the worst news of a tragic death. It was my dad asking if I would help distribute political flyers for the upcoming 1960 election. I corralled Doug Carnine to help me and we went door-to-door after school. We picked up the flyers at Nichol's law office. I think my dad always regretted asking us to do this; it just wasn't a proper thing to do.

⤳

Orson Moorehead was a town cop, which in a town like Tuscola, usually meant the one to start parades and look official. When he boarded at our house when I was very young, I never paid attention, but later I realized that Orson was an institution in Tuscola. In a town like Tuscola, he was all the comfort we needed. I remember asking my parents if Orson was married. They said his wife lived in Decatur. I never quite understood why he lived in our house and his wife lived 45 miles away.

I suppose having Orson rent a room and live with us added some security, although it was not really needed. He was the town policeman, even though sometimes in the manner of a Barney Fife rather than Andy Taylor. Even if some people may have thought of him that way, he was still a reassuring presence and loved the schoolkids. Crime didn't exist, at least anything more serious than someone who had too much to drink out at the tavern east of town near Camargo. Tuscola was a dry town—other than the Moose Lodge on Saturday night—but that was way down south on Highway 36, so that was out of my worldly orbit.

One of the few of my pre-school memories involved Orson. On Christmas Eve one year, I was standing at the head of the stairs, in an anticipatory state for the next morning. The Christmas tree, the repository of all my forthcoming presents was downstairs and I was anxiously awaiting Santa. I heard a noise downstairs, something like a thump or crash. Mom said "go to bed, it must be Orson coming in late." I hollered for Orson, but no reply. It had to be Santa. To this day, I never knew what it was, but at the time, I was convinced it was Santa. What else?

～

Having a hometown with a long history of the family also meant having teachers that my parents had. Even though Dad was 42 and Mom 34 when I was born, we still shared teachers. Miss Sluss taught me Latin and she was so old to my 14-year-old eyes, I figured she probably spoke Latin in ancient Rome. I don't know of any high school now that teaches Latin, but I have always found it useful in understanding English. I guess it has gone the way of home-ec and other subjects modern schools find of no use.

Miss Deer (why were the female teachers usually "old maids," to use the term we used then?), taught my folks, brother, and me biology, which I found to be the basis of my entire career. Dad told stories of his loving to dissect frogs and other slimy samples that the girls quivered and quailed over in class. Seeing his picture as a very handsome high school senior, I can see why he might have been the teacher's pet of those "old maid" teachers. Except for Bertha Flack of course.

I heard many times Dad's high school travails with his teacher Bertha Flack. Miss Flack favored the girls (according to Dad), so any boy got the short end of the stick. Actually, I kind of like that reverse discrimination, but Dad had problems with it. His class right before hers was PE, far across the building, and requiring a quick shower afterward. He often was a minute or two late to her class. It got to where she would lock the door to keep him out. He complained to the principal, who promptly told Miss Flack to give him some leeway. This only made matters worse. He said he got even years later, when he was on the coal rationing board during WWII and he refused her extra coal which she needed to heat her very large house; he chuckled rather evilly—quite out of character for him—when he recounted this story to me decades later. I wish I could go back and stand silently and hear her click the lock and hear him go slowly down to the principal to complain. He got in, but not as any favorite of Miss Flack. A different kind of sexual harassment, indeed.

❧

Tuscola had a famous resident in the guise of Frog or Smiley Burnette. When grain dealer James Bush formed the third radio station in the United States in the late '20s—the 100-watt WDZ in Tuscola—he meant for it to announce grain prices. In 1929 he hired 18-year-old Lester Burnett to be the only on-air employee. Burnett worked from 6 in the morning to 6 in the evening and did everything, including playing music on some of the eventual 100 instruments he played and even invented. After reading the grain prices, he would read comics, using a different voice for many characters. One character took hold. He adopted the name Smiley, from Mark Twain's 1865 short story *The Celebrated Jumping Frog of Calaveras County*. Twain's character Jim Smiley had a pet frog, so Burnett became Smiley, later adding an e to Burnette, and later nicknamed Frog.

In 1933, Gene Autry found out that a radio personality in downstate Illinois played music, so he called Smiley and asked if he wanted to come work with him on the National Barn Dance on the world's largest radio station, WLS in Chicago. Gene asked how much Smiley was making and was told $12.50 a week. Gene said he could offer $35 a week plus expenses and asked Smiley to think it over. Smiley replied quickly "I've thunk it over. How far away are you?" Thus ended Smiley's career in Tuscola and began a long career as Autry's sidekick which included 64 movies. Their last movies were made in 1953, about the time Tuscola kids started remembering Smiley visiting Tuscola and the schools. He always considered Mrs. Bush as "Mommie Bush" and visited them often at their home on Sale Street, across from the Methodist church.

As Bob Rogers recollected, "Whenever Smiley would visit the Bushes he would make the rounds of all the schools to see the kids. We all knew him and he remembered some of our names, too, which was a pretty big deal at the time. He would talk with us about right, wrong, respect, honor, and how important family was. He would get right in there and play whatever game we were playing at recess, and just be a nice human being. Besides spending time with us he always had pictures to sign and give away. I had a photo of Smiley and Black Eyed Nellie, his horse. What made Smiley special to us was that he was a Saturday matinee star who was our real-life friend."

Donna Ard remembered Smiley, too. "I remember coming out of school at the North Ward and Smiley Burnette was giving out pictures of him and his horse Ring Eye, autographed." And Betty Powell Holcomb shared that, "One time, when my dad and I were downtown (I think going into Gus's) we ran into Smiley. He autographed some kind of a paper or card and drew a little frog on it for me."

I cannot remember ever seeing Smiley but I probably did. Regardless, many people in Tuscola have very fond memories of Smiley, as do old-timers from around the world. Smiley was one-of-a-kind who unfortunately is hard to find nowadays. But he typifies what Tuscola was about. It was about friends and heroes, parents and teachers and a bond that never tears apart.

⌘

Rosie Cler had his "store" next to my dad's Corn Belt office on Sale Street downtown. I often went to see my dad at work, but never went inside Rosie's. Just walking by was an experience, so I asked classmates to share their recollections.

Donna Ard Braden recounted her impressions of Rosie's: "You would almost need a picture to describe what it looked like from the outside. Merchandise nailed and hanging on the wall, going up to second story. Had to walk around the walk as it was always piled high in front. Inside was dark, dingy with wood floors. No order, total chaos, but Rosie knew what and where things were. Looking back, it was a horrible eye sore for Sale Street. Having said that, I went in there a few times with my dad when I was younger. I am sure that was through my mother's objections as Rosie was not considered the pillar of Sale Street! If I had to describe it, I would call it a junk yard with walls. Lots of iron work and rubber hose. If Dad needed something fabricated on the farm machinery, Rosie was where he went. Once I went in with Dad and I had my hula hoop with me. Dad told him I was so good, I could hula any size he could make. A couple days later, Rosie came to our house with a round black hose that was about 6' diameter to see if I could hula it! When I did, he left the hose with me, and may have lost a bet with dad. This recollection is through the eyes of a young 8 or 9 year old girl."

Mike Carroll added: "Rosie Cler's shop sold plumbing and heating and general construction supplies. It was a holy disorganized mess: stuff on floor, hanging from ceiling, etc. You could barely walk through it. It was amazing they sold anything, but, Rosie was one of Tuscola's famous "characters" and people liked to go in and visit him and listen to his stories. Most of us who remember Rosie's think of the theme for Huey's, a similar store in Urbana at Five Points. It sold junk like Rosie's. Their theme was: "If it ain't on the shelf, it's on the wall. If it ain't on the wall it's on the floor. If it ain't on the floor, it's on the ceiling. If it ain't on the ceiling, you don't need it." When us old timers think of Rosies, we think of this theme from Huey's."

TWELVE

ERVIN PARK

B ORDERED ON THE west by railroad tracks, and cornfields on the north and east, the broad expanse of open space
at the north end of Tuscola is Ervin Park. I first knew it as I
tagged along with my dad who managed a Little League team
in the early '50s. The north half was ball diamonds and the
remnants of the old stage and amphitheater. The south half
of the Park contained the playground equipment. I remember
playing on the swings and the old fashioned metal slide and
merry-go-round.

Who was Ervin? No one ever asked this, although I am sure
he was a generous pioneer of this town, now long departed and
forgotten. Except he will live forever in the trees and swings
and baseball diamonds, tennis courts, swimming pool—and
memories—for generations of children and adults.

Summer was filled with the endless sound of cicadas
and the sweltering Illinois August heat. For many evenings, I
watched the sun drop beyond the horizon as uniformed boys
played Little League baseball. For me, it was a tradition that
lays as heavy as the humid air. Six innings were rushed to a
finish before the fading light ended. There were no artificial
lights—we played by nature's rules. Games were called for
darkness when the pitching was bad or the hitting was good.

Countless baseballs were fouled past the left-field line
across the park road and into the cornfield. My expertise was
crawling under the wire fence to find them. This was easy in
early July but became difficult by mid-August. I am sure many

Rawlings baseballs still rot under the fertile humus, now covered by houses, the corn a long-lost memory.

I will forever hear the thunder of the eight o'clock Illinois Central—the City of New Orleans—racing south from Chicago, bound for a distant and magical place in an unknown land.

The old amphitheater was in ruins at the far north end of the Park. We played on the concrete seating supports; the sad remnants meant nothing to me, but to my parents' generation, they were skeletons of long ago vaudeville shows and Saturday night dances.

My generation witnessed the birth of the swimming pool and the tennis courts. The old amphitheater was bulldozed and cleared to make room for a new baseball diamond and a small covered picnic area. And I grew too old to bother with swings and teeter-totters; suddenly that was for little kids. A new generation came to play and ride bicycles. I listened to the music revolution of the Sixties as I watched fellow teenagers wax their newly washed cars on Saturday afternoons in the shade of catalpa trees. New trees were planted and the old ones where I once hung from branches were removed as hazardous.

The last time I visited Ervin Park was over twenty years ago. Walking as a middle-aged man on a cold, windy winter day, I tried to see what I remembered but instead saw new ball diamonds with lights, and a new golf course to the north where cornfields still held onto my memory. I looked now at million-dollar homes in the golf course subdivision, and houses where I crawled under a fence to retrieve foul balls lost in the corn.

The City of New Orleans still raced past every evening. Boys rode bicycles and carried baseball gloves. Young mothers, the children of my classmates, tended their young on plastic slides and new swings that met safety standards unknown in my day. The faces are different, as is the music and cars. The dreams of an unknown future are there, but not mine. My dreams were replaced by memories. Both the dreams and memories bring smiles. The echoes of laughter bounce off the amphitheater stage. The crack of baseballs on ash bats fades into the humid night air. The stalks of corn reach deep into the black soil. Who has heard of Stan Musial or Al Kaline? I wore their gloves and swung their bats.

Ervin Park is still there, standing through July thunderstorms and December blizzards. The catalpa trees still shed their bean pods. I walk the road by myself. No one walks anymore. And the bats are aluminum. And I still ask who Mr. Ervin was. I want to thank him.

PHOTO GALLERY

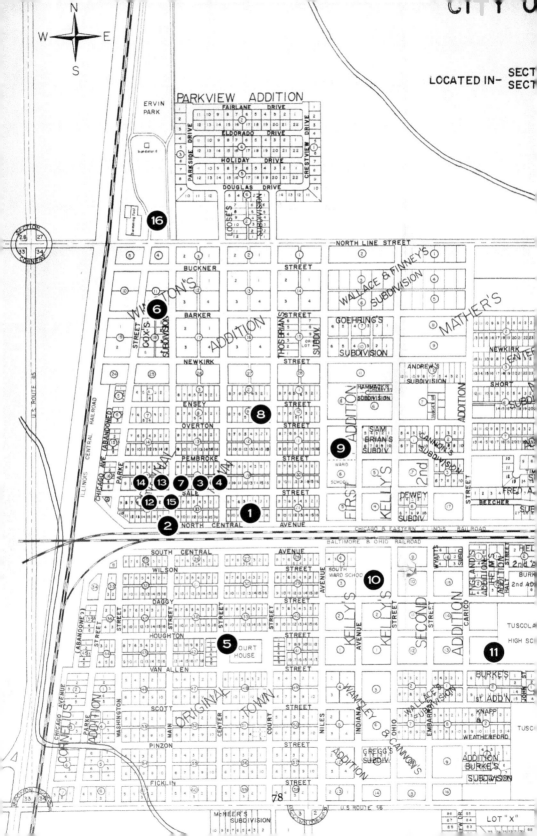

MAP OF TUSCOLA 1961

Key to Locations

1. 204 E.N. Central Avenue.
2. Intersection of Main Street and North Central Avenue.
3. Library.
4. Post Office.
5. Court House.
6. Jarman Hospital.
7. Hotel Douglas.
8. Old North Ward School.
9. New North Ward School.
10. South Ward School.
11. Tuscola Community High School.
12. Strand Theater.
13. Ben Franklin Variety Store.
14. Corn Belt Building and Loan (Colwell Agency).
15. Gus's.
16. Ervin Park.

Top: R.B. (Raleigh) Colwell (1905-2002) in the Corn Belt Building and Loan office, West Sale Street, probably 1930s or 40s.

Right: Ruby Hance Colwell (1913-1993), the first Miss Tuscola, 1932. Runner up in the Miss Illinois contest. Bathing suit belonged to Henry Senn.

Opposite

Top: Author with dog Wiggles on his snow mountain in front of 204 E.N. Central Avenue.

Bottom: Downtown Tuscola, circa 1960, looking north on Main Street at intersection with North Central Avenue.

Top: Carnegie Library, East Sale
Street, Tuscola, circa 1940.

Bottom: U.S. Post Office, East Sale
Street, Tuscola, Illinois. Circa 1940s.

Top: Mural inside Tuscola Post Office, by artist Edwin Boyd Johnson, 1941.

Bottom: Court House, Douglas County, Tuscola, Illinois, circa 1960.

Top: Jarman Hospital.
Boomers born here were called
Jarman babies.

Bottom: Hotel Douglas on
corner of Sale and Main Streets.
Destroyed by fire, 1975.

North Side Public School, Tuscola, Ill. 48606-R

Top: Petro, or USI, west of Tuscola on US Route 36, circa 1960.

Bottom: The Old North Ward Grade School, where author and classmates attended grades 1-4. Torn down late 1950s.

Top: Third grade class taught by Bess Bundy, 1956, in front of old North Ward. Author front row, second from right.

Bottom: New North Ward/Old High School. Built on Sale and Niles Street after fire destroyed the old Union School. When new high school was built in 1957, this was converted to New North Ward Grade School. Demolished in early 2000s

Opposite

Top: South Ward Grade School on South Niles Street. Built after fire destroyed the old Union School. Torn down in 1990s.

Bottom: Tuscola High School on East Prairie Street. Built in 1957-58. First graduating class in May, 1959, of which author's brother Ron was a member.

SOUTH SIDE GRADE SCHOOL TUSCOLA ILL. L-391

Top: Entrance to Ervin Park, Main and North Line Streets. 1960.

Bottom: Little League Yankees circa 1950. Author, back left, holding the hand of his dad, Coach R.B. Colwell. Author's brother Ron, kneeling, third from left.

Opposite

Top: Author in midst of assembling high school biology class leaf collection, sophomore year, 1963.

Bottom: The Strand Theater, West Sale Street, Tuscola.

21. Right: Author posing in Tuscola High band uniform in front yard of 204 E.N.Central Avenue, with Stella Cullison's thorny bushes and house in background.

Bottom: TCHS Band Director Carl Kohrt.

The vice president was accompanied by his wife, Pat.

Top: Author in center, with Halloween costume. Keigley sisters, next door neighbors.

Bottom: Richard and Pat Nixon on whistle stop campaign tour fall of 1960. On Illinois Central tracks, west edge of Tuscola.

Top: Tuscola High School class of
1965 assembled on football field
for yearbook photo, October 1964.

Bottom: 50th reunion of Tuscola
High School class of 1965.

PART II

꙯

A Time: Mid-Century

The time was the mid-twentieth century—the 1950s and early 1960s. The old saying "you had to be there" applies to this story. I was born in 1947 and my generation was described as "Baby Boomers." Due to the post-World War II population increase, the grade schools hired extra teachers and dedicated more classrooms. Perhaps that precipitated the building of a new high school, tearing down of the old North Ward, and conversion of the old high school to replace the North Ward Grade School. From what I remember, we seemed to think ourselves special—Greatest Class Alive. Looking back a half-century, that time was indeed different. The world itself was different and that reflected on the life we lived—only a few years after the Big War, which followed on the heels of the Great Depression. Our parents were influenced by these events and that reflected on their children.

I am sure every grade level and generation thinks they are special—and every grade level and generation is correct. We live in a world slightly different from our parents, our siblings, and our children. The foundation of our lives is shaped by our childhood. Our childhood is shaped and molded not only by the place but the time. Family and friends, schools and churches, playgrounds, and the streets and buildings form lasting memories. Time flows like water down a river. It disappears around the bend but continues to flow. We can walk downstream, trying to find it, just as we try to recall memories—the time that has drifted over the horizon.

THIRTEEN

TUSCOM LITTLE LEAGUE

THE SMALL SLEEPY town surrounded by corn and bean fields simmered in the sultry heat of an early Illinois August. The year was 1959. A decade was ending. I was twelve years old, and this was my final year of wearing the ABC Yankees Little League uniform—the American Business Club Yankees. I had no idea who the American Business Club was. Obviously, they supported the team financially, and I do believe they got their money's worth. Originally the team was the Moose Yankees— sponsored by the Moose Lodge; I would have preferred to be a "Moose" rather than an ABC Yankee. We wore tailor-made green caps; and the uniform with the elastic band around the ankles, a little short to showcase those big white socks with green stripes that came up over the knees. The whole ensemble spoke power and prestige and I stood minutes at a time in front of a mirror on game days. My dad was a coach, and as horrible a player as I was, I doubt if I could have made any other team.

A Yankee. It was inconceivable that I could have been part of the red-capped Rotary Indians or purple Knights of Columbus Cardinals. I think the blue-capped VFW Cubs rounded out the lot. Central Illinois was sort of a Mason Dixon split. We were equal distance from Chicago and St. Louis, and being a big-league Cardinal fan or a Cub fan told a lot about a person. The New York Yankees were, of course, a universal favorite; as winning teams usually were. Mickey Mantle was my hero until the day lightning hit our TV antenna and fried the TV just a split second after Mickey swished air on a strike three that lost a game on a stormy Saturday game-of-the-week. I was so disillusioned I figured the lightning was a sign from above that maybe I better change allegiance and go with my dad and brother as a diehard Cardinal fan.

But I was 12 and my baseball career was soon to end. Tuscom—as in Tuscola Community Little League—taught 8-year-old boys the finer aspects of sports and refined that experience for 4 or 5 years. Thirteen-year-olds could graduate into Pony League, but things got serious then

In my entire career in that wonderful uniform, I had only two hits. Oh, I remember those vividly. They both came at the twilight of my career. I rarely swung the bat, but for good reasons. The obvious was I could never hit the ball. In practice, I would stand there for agonizingly long minutes swinging air as my dad patiently pitched easy balls at me. He held his disappointment as my teammates realized this was an easy time to catch up on gossip.

The second reason had to do with my size. I was small for my age and my dad, in his wisdom of baseball strategy, knew a small boy crouching in a bent-over stance my mother thought cute, would narrow the strike zone to something that would crowd a butterfly. This was my dad's desperation move. It only occurred when the Yankees were in desperate straits. Think of it, the bottom of the 6th (we only played 6 innings) and the Yankees trailed by one run. Mike Allen led off with a single. Next was Richard Lindsey, then Dennis Scheu. Time for "Little Joe." I'm at the end of the bench day dreaming; I'm swinging my legs in a circular motion left to right.

"Joe!"

Did I hear something in the fog? I'm riding my bicycle chasing after Glenda. Did she look back and call my name?

"Joe!!"

No, that wasn't Glenda.

"Joe. Get up to the plate!!!"

Whoa, it's my dad. He wants me.

"Get a walk. Jimmy is up next. Be ready to run like a rabbit if he gets a hit."

A walk?! This could be my chance to get a hit!

"Remember, crouch down."

OK, I can do that. Moans slowly rise from the pitcher as he sees the "little Joe" ploy. My teammates all give me encouraging chatter.

"Get a walk, Joe. Lean down. Hey pitcher, get a magnifying glass for the strike zone. Go get em, Joe."

"Ball one."

Man, what a long way to first.

"Ball three."

What? I don't remember ball two. Should I have swung at that one?

"Don't swing at it, Joe."

"Ball four."

Oh boy, now the pressure is on. I don't want to be here on base. What if Jimmy gets a hit? Everyone is watching me. Should I run? They might catch me in a run down. I don't know how to do this. I could lose the game. What if it's a fly ball? Do I run or stand still? Why put this pressure on a little kid? And so it went.

⌇

The worst part was when it wasn't the bottom of the 6th. A few times I had to play defense. Right field. Right field was where they always put types like me. There were few lefties or switch hitters; few batters could place their hits. Thank goodness. Just luck of the swing. And not that many swings took balls to right field. Plus we usually had a wide-ranging center fielder. But I didn't escape humiliation out there either. My fear of being on base was nothing compared to the terror of right field. Oh, I was proud standing there before the first batter came to the

97

plate. I was playing. After all, I was familiar with the view from there. I usually was the one who raised the flag as the record player scratched out the national anthem. Everyone would watch me, in my neat uniform, raising the flag.

At first, there was just one ball diamond for Little League. With only four teams, we didn't need more. We had no lights, so we toughed out the shrinking daylight of late summer evenings. We did call a few games due to darkness, but those were usually the 21-17 score games. Games started at 6 p.m., and by 8:00 we were squinting into the sunset.

Crickets and cicadas serenaded the hazy, sultry nights. We watched the building thunderstorms, often scurrying to pack things as the sky opened up just as we got the third out in the bottom of the 6th. I can still hear the distant thunder and the lonely whistle of the 8:15 freight rumbling down the Illinois Central tracks.

One ball field and four teams: the ABC Yankees, VFW Cubs, Rotary Indians, and Knights of Columbus Cardinals. The Yankees hated the Indians. They must have been good. Then, at some point, we added teams. And the town grew. We built a second diamond. That made life more complicated. Two games per evening. That was progress, but I think we lost something in the bargain.

Ervin Park was up to the challenge though. There was room for expansion. The old amphitheater at the north end of the Park was rundown and covered with weeds, crumbling along with the memories of a turn of the century small town. Its memories were bulldozed and the second ball diamond was built.

So went my Little League career. Tuscola in the summer. Ervin Park. Little League. I was proud to be a Yankee and there was no greater joy than to put on that uniform. We too often lose touch of what it is all about to grow up. Winning isn't everything. It's learning to feel good, even if that requires rationalization. And a little daydreaming. Just don't let other people down. It must have broken my dad's heart, and quite possibly added to his already graying hair that I was no match for just about everyone else my age, and four years younger. But he overlooked it. He lived for baseball in a way I will never know or understand.

Dad was a legend in the early days of Little League. I wasn't, but Little League was a staple in our family and part of Tuscola for pre-teen boys. Few of us who wore the uniforms will ever forget. Nightly games and daily practice were the first lessons in sportsmanship, teamwork, pride, playful razzing and complaining about umpires. Raymond Lee as umpire, coaches Harold Sheu, Bob Hastings, the Conners, Irv Eaton, Jack Wellons—the names continue past my ability to remember. But they were there for the young boys. Some of the boys continued into high school and college sports; some, like me, became fans. But all carried into adulthood the values so many instilled in us. "Play ball" is an anthem we all remember.

In the years since I last took off the Yankee green, I returned many times to the diamonds. Usually in a cold November wind, under cloudy looming skies. Preferably by myself.

In those later visits, I stood silently and listened. Some people just hear the wind. I hear the cries of "get a walk, Joe." The pounding of fists in Al Kaline mitts, the scratchy record playing the *Star-Spangled Banner* as I pulled the ropes raising the flag—they are familiar and comforting sounds. I smell the warm evening air as Tom Grubb nails Greg Skinner trying to slide into home as strike 3 whizzes past Bill Englehardt; the shouts and applause as Butch Consoer lays one over the fence to lead off the 4th. And the tinny voice over the whining loudspeaker as official scorekeeper Ron Colwell announces "and Danny Deaver steps up to the plate, sporting a .233 batting average with 10 RBIs, 15 strikeouts and 1 home run." The fading echoes of the crowd ring in my ears as the freight train rumbles down the IC headed south towards Memphis and New Orleans.

This cold, late-20th-century November wind has circled the globe thousands of times since those days. It has blown snow off Antarctic glaciers, massaged the backs of humpbacked whales lolling off Baja, and carried the sands of the Sahara into the ruins of ancient Greek temples. But it still carries the smell of a fresh new Rawlins Little League baseball and the sound of a Hillerich and Bradsby Stan Musial 30" bat knocking against a 32" Lou Gehrig in the canvas carrying sack.

A shaft of sunlight glistens off a November snowflake, taking me back to July cornstalks, the catalpa trees, reflections off the fins of a red '59 Plymouth, and the green of the Yankee uniform—with its ABC patch. The Stars and Stripes—a new one that year, with 50 stars, will forever flap from the flagpole in center field as green and purple uniforms line up and salute.

They may add lights, they may allow aluminum bats, they may add concrete bleachers and an electric scoreboard. Those things are fleeting. They fade as the cold November wind brings back the real essence of Tuscola of 1959, Ervin Park, and the final year of Little League to a 12-year-old boy in a world that no longer exists.

FOURTEEN

MUSHROOMS

THE WINDS OF March brought the promise of April green for a young boy in Tuscola. "April showers bring May flowers," our mothers said as a way to justify our staying indoors when it rained. The spring rains brought an explosion of green on the maple and ash trees, tulips, and lawns to be mowed. It also brought morel mushrooms.

My dad had mushroom hunted for decades, and knew exactly where to go. He took me on the trips to the river bottom woods and the railroad rights-of-way—places that spoke of excitement and adventure to a young boy. I would walk along daydreaming when he would stop and say he smelled them. I would look around and see nothing. Then I noticed I was standing in the middle of a patch of dozens. I believed him, trusting as only a nine-year-old can.

We drove southeast of town to the woodlands along the Embarras River. It was not far from town, but to me, it was a forest wilderness—trees and tangles and treasures of the unknown. And mushrooms.

The mushrooms sometimes migrated a little from year to year. No matter—he knew where they would be. This was his home for decades—he grew up with these and similar woods. Maybe he did smell them. When we found one mushroom, we found dozens. They covered the forest floor, hidden amongst mayapples and skunk cabbage. I picked the morels as if they might disappear before my very eyes. We filled grocery sacks full. I came home the proud discoverer, the bags of furrowed spongy mushrooms held tightly in my hands.

I anxiously waited for Mom to heat the skillet, sizzling with butter. Real butter, not margarine. Then she would roll the mushrooms in flour and carefully put in the hot pan, probably the much loved cast iron skillet she gave my wife as a wedding present fifty years ago.

I never got enough. I could live forever as a nine-year-old on morels. I probably could as a 70-year-old, but sadly, I have not eaten a morel in decades. Back then, we needed nothing else for dinner. Several more trips to the woods, then the mushrooms were gone. Springtime meant mushrooms for a short time, brown treasures among the green of the forest floor.

The railroad rights-of-way meant not only morels but also wild asparagus. As only a nine-year-old can stubbornly do, I turned up my nose. Mom loved these more than mushrooms. I could see them, their weedy spears sticking up through old leaves. Probably without ever tasting one, I turned them down. My loss. I savor them now, cooked like the shrooms in butter, although we usually steam them al dente.

As with the morels, Dad could "smell" them. I ran along the tracks, anxiously looking for mushrooms, oblivious to anything but the freedom of the rails. "You passed some. I can smell them." Sure enough, when I looked closer, they were there. Doubtfully, I pressed my nose to the plant. There was no smell—how could he smell them? I didn't see the gleam in his eye and a slight smile as he looked up in the sky. Then he would say something like "it also smells like rain. We better head home." He had gardened since before he was my age and knew the ways of plants. Also, he knew the ways of gullible young boys.

I think back to the sunny April days so long ago and in a different world than now. The robins and cardinals greeted the warm mornings as storm clouds appeared over Illinois skies. It has been well over half a century. Dad and Mom are long gone as are Illinois skies for me. I will never again find morel mushrooms in the oak and sycamore forests down by the river.

The mushrooms were tasty and wonderful—they still are in my memory—so delicious to me was the freedom, the feeling of being part of the wild. Also, the freedom of childhood, under the safe and watchful eyes of parents. That freedom of the wild was only the beginning for me—a desire of the unknown and untamed. Now, I enjoy the freedom of the past, looking for hidden treasures, surrounded by safety, teased by the future.

Springtime will always be morel mushrooms, Dad leading me through river bottom woods, finding them by smell, beaming with pride as I filled bags with them. Dad and Mom live now only in my mind as do the smells of mushrooms sizzling on the stovetop.

FIFTEEN

THUNDERSTORM

Mornings were usually hot in August in Tuscola. I was accustomed to steamy summer days with muggy air clogging the lungs. The sky a hazy blue—a blue I thought was normal. The sky ended on a horizon which was not very far away. In 1959, I had not become accustomed to the Western crystal clear bluebird sky that ends in craggy peaks or distant ridges; that was yet to come.

Blue jays scolded my world from treetops on E.N. Central Avenue. Elm and maple and ash trees lined the streets of my neighborhood. We may not have had the endless forests I had encountered during family vacations west, but Tuscola did have an assortment of trees I would later display in my leaf collection in high school for Dorothy Deer's biology class. The variety of "shade trees" eclipsed the non-diverse conifer forests I later explored, and managed, too.

On sultry days, the cicadas filled the air with sound waves muffled through the dampness. Or they could have been crickets and other bug things that intrigued my inquisitiveness concerning things natural. I was fascinated by the shapes and sizes and colors of the little things that crawled or flew.

By the afternoon, the stillness competed with the stifling heat. I could feel the storm coming, ominous and threatening. It saturated my senses as it saturated the air. Off to the west, as much as one could see very far west, it appeared as mountains of cloud. Building, boiling, roiling upwards. White turning to grey to blue, then purple, it filled the sky. It filled my being as well as my imagination.

The attack was sudden, with short warning. Sometimes the TV put a little symbol on the bottom of the screen. But in those days, who watched TV on an August afternoon? I looked up in the darkening sky, awed by cloud tops stretching halfway to the moon. But there was no moon. The lightning lit the backsides of the dark clouds. The wind hit with the force of one of those fast freights of the Baltimore & Ohio railroad.

Birds streaked by, turned and hovered, wings outstretched in the gale. They knew no fear. They did know the wind. Branches swayed, leaves broke loose, chasing the birds. Dirt and candy wrappers swept over the ground.

The first raindrops pattered slowly, then quickened. It was fun to stand head turned upwards catching a raindrop. But when they started hitting my eyes, the fun ended. I knew when to run inside. Pumping as fast as I could on my bicycle, I flew with the birds, racing them to get home and inside. The blackening sky brought a sense of panic.

Safely inside, I stood wide-eyed as lightning and its thunder echoes filled the house. Looking out the window, I saw rain coming in buckets, pounding, splashing. Puddles appeared suddenly as rivers ran along the streets and sidewalks.

A sudden flash lit the world I was watching, with the boom of thunder almost at the same time. The power went off as a tree fell across a power line somewhere in town. The thunder still echoed in my head as I laughed, covering the fear I felt. Was this how Noah felt, I wondered? Rain turned to hail, which signaled the end. The ice pellets bounced off the roof, deafening me almost as much as the thunder.

I stood expectant as the sky lightened, the wind eased. The fading pitter-patter of light raindrops turned to drips from the trees. Thunder faded east, trailing a lighter grey of thinning clouds. Sunlight broke through in a blue sky, bringing cool air with an ozone-cleansed freshness. It was time to ease my way outside, sidestepping the still flowing street-rivers. Puddles were almost swimming pools.

Birds reappeared from their hidden sanctuaries, invigorated by the cool air. Crickets who had been silenced slowly began their serenades. Already the nightcrawlers were covering the ground, wriggling and splaying themselves in drowned pity on the sidewalks. Today's baseball game was obviously rained out due to the mud, so I went to the nearby South Ward schoolyard, exploring damage of downed trees and limbs.

Just another August thunderstorm on another summer day, providing more sultry humidity for tomorrow. We gathered branches to pile in the alley. Dad had to wait for the mud to dry so he could work in the garden. Tomatoes needed to be picked and the weeds that would shoot up overnight needed to be pulled. A normal summer day for a twelve-year-old—a memory that doesn't let go with the passage of time.

SIXTEEN

DECORATION DAY

ONE OF AMERICA'S formal holidays. Officially the calendar labeled it Memorial Day, but we all knew it as Decoration Day, the day we decorated the graves in the cemetery. May 30—every year—it occurred one day after my birthday. This was before bureaucrats made it part of a three-day weekend—varying by date every year and losing its true meaning.

The holiday signaled the start of summer since it usually occurred within a day or two of the last day of school. It was the climax of May, which was the climax of springtime in Illinois. The peony bushes honored us by opening their sweet flowers, always covered by ants. A row of peonies bloomed on the west side of our yard, next to Cullison's house. That is until Mrs. Cullison tired of me and my friends stepping over her property line to retrieve baseballs, footballs or whatever landed near her house. She planted a row of thorny bushes that only stimulated us to intentionally throw things over there. The peonies disappeared.

Memorial Day was created to honor war dead, but while we were doing that, we went ahead and honored all those resting beneath gravestones. We entered the cemetery in hushed tones. I never gave a thought about death and those resting there. But I knew it was a somber occasion requiring a serious attitude. No running around, no loud noises, no laughing. We would pick our way through lots of flowers and baskets, placed by other somber people walking with heads down until we found the markers we were looking for.

My mother's parents were there, people I never knew. My mother's father died before I was born and her mother soon after I was born. Thus, unlike many kids my age, I didn't know the meaning of grandparent. From pictures and stories, I doubt if I would have liked them, but grandparents in those days were different from today. Struggle to survive on a farm, raise a dozen or half dozen children while trying to eke out a living, and for some reason, grandparents didn't care to spend time with another batch of kids.

There was usually a parade and men with fold-up hats and patches that said VFW or American Legion who carried rifles and seemed to be somber as well. I cringed when they raised their guns and fired them in the air. At a prescribed time, someone hidden behind a mausoleum in the cemetery played taps. I was glad when all this seriousness was over so we could go home, and Dad would make ice cream in the little wooden barrel with the electric motor.

When I was in high school, I was in the marching band in the parade. We played a few songs, then the top cornet player slinked off behind the mausoleum to play taps. Gary Forrester did it for a couple of years, then Tom McDaniel inherited the top spot. I think our minds were elsewhere since we were out of step and out of tune more than usual. This was always the last appearance of the year for the band since school was soon out.

When I left home to go to college, my experiences with Memorial Day quickly changed. The last 3-day weekend in May was institutionalized, and became more memorable as the weekend of the Indianapolis 500 race. Things were being rearranged all over the place to fit people's desires, none of which centered on honoring the dead or the meanings behind traditions. My opinions about death also changed. I saw cemeteries as a waste of space, and the idea of pumping bodies full of formaldehyde to keep them from doing what nature intended, to be a reprehensible practice. I didn't go into cemeteries any longer, other than to visit old ones in mountain mining towns for historical reasons. I never went back to the Tuscola cemetery except to bury my mother in 1993, then my father in 2002. I haven't been back since. And I have never placed flowers on any grave. Not out of disrespect; I often think of my parents. But I don't think of them lying in a coffin sealed in a vault, awaiting that day they expected to be lifted by a Jesus with upraised arms. I think of them as I knew them as a kid. So much for the somber and serious attitude of a ten-year-old witnessing Decoration Day.

We probably lost something when we mistook the holiday of remembrance for a holiday to go to the beach or the mountains or family reunions where "Uncle Bob" grills hamburgers and hotdogs. We have lost many things since those good-old-days of mid-century. Maybe if more of us honored a Decoration Day with the celebration of youth and the mentors of our youth, we might be a little better off. Traditions are there for reasons. When we forget the reasons, there are no longer traditions.

SEVENTEEN

SUMMER NIGHTS
AND DAYS

FIREFLIES DOTTED THE August nights with their flickering flashes of light. The year was 1956. I was nine years old and knew nothing else about how to spend a sweltering, muggy summer evening. We sat outside on the front steps, watching the remnants of twilight fade into dark blue. It was too hot to be inside. Air conditioning was only something experienced in movie theaters or fancy places we didn't frequent. We cooled off, as it were, by sitting outside, hopefully in an evening breeze, watching fireflies and taking in the evening sounds of crickets, cicadas, and far off dogs barking. If we waited, we would watch and listen to the eastbound freight roaring by on the railroad tracks across the street.

Our neighbors were lucky. They all had front porches they could relax on. Our porch was enclosed, so to be outside, we had to huddle on the concrete steps or else lie on the grass. There was plenty to pay attention to. Far off to the west, toward Decatur, we could see what we called heat lightning. The towering thunderstorms were winding down for the evening. We would probably not get any rain from this one. But I was fascinated by the brightness that backlit the thunderhead cloud. Not knowing any different, I believed my folks that this was a different kind of lightning that had no thunder with it. It was caused by this hot weather. Magic of some kind. Just like the lightning bugs that carried their own flashlights. To a nine-year-old, the world was full of magic.

I had no set bedtime, although I didn't have one during the school year either. I usually set my own schedules and my folks trusted me. On these hot nights, I was in no hurry to lay in bed, on top of the covers, too hot to sleep. My bedroom contained the huge window fan. Dad would turn it on as soon as the outside air was cooler than the inside. Usually, sometime in the middle of the night, he would tiptoe in and turn it off. I somehow fell asleep with the sound of an airplane engine five feet away. I did enjoy the wind blowing by my head. Once in a while, the rain would come and the fan would suck in the raindrops before one of us could shut the fan off and lower the window.

I don't remember specific discussions or conversations while sitting outside in the humid night air. Most hot nights, all four of us sat outside. We might talk about the latest Little League game, or church events, or family stories. Or we would use our energy to try and cool off. Funny how memories recall the little things like the fireflies or heat lightning but dismiss most else.

The July and August days were more sweltering than the nights, but when that is all you know, it is normal. In later years, when I was used to the very dry heat of the West, I would occasionally travel back to Tuscola in the summer. I thought I would die from the steam heat. The western 90-degree heat I was used to with its 15% humidity was easily tolerated. The mid-Illinois 90/90 combination was intolerable. How could people live in this I wondered. When I was nine and had never experienced low humidity, there was nothing unusual about this torture.

But the nights! A reprieve of coolness was nice, as were the thunderstorms that often swept through at 2 a.m. or 3 a.m. I remember one afternoon, a bright flash with an immediate clap of thunder told us we were close to a strike. Later that evening, I walked two blocks north and saw a huge old maple split to the ground by lightning. On the former prairie like we were, the trees and houses of town attracted the bolts of electricity.

Besides the hot nights and fireflies, we did contemplate what the summer had brought. August was the culmination of the summer. Labor Day marked the beginning of school, Little League was finished by early August, tomatoes were ripe, and the freedom of summer was approaching its end. The anticipation of a new teacher, a few new students in a class of old friends, maybe a different school building, maybe a couple of new shirts or pairs of pants, all this combined to a climax in August.

Since my dad coached Little League, that tied us to Tuscola until baseball season was over. Only then could we take our annual vacation. Early on, we were pioneers to the wilds of Minnesota. We would stay in a cabin, no camping for us, and fish and swim and visit the tourist attractions of Nisswa or Ely. One year we visited the headwaters of the Mississippi at Lake Itasca, the statues of Paul Bunyan, the Indian curio shops. But the mainstay was fishing for Dad. My brother and I never took to fishing, which I am sure greatly disappointed Dad. Mom spent her time cleaning the fish and cooking them, and Ron and I swam, boated, or just lay around.

I look at the old photos of us smiling and swimming, Dad holding the pike and walleye, sometimes as large as me. Mom favored the bluegill and perch and I occasionally would catch one, but I was too impatient. And put a wriggling worm on a hook? Forget it. Even with that, somehow I ended up getting a college degree in wildlife management. Go figure.

There were infrequent interruptions in our northern excursions, as we headed west instead. I looked forward to driving to Boulder, Colorado, to visit Uncle Chuck and Aunt Mabel. She was my favorite aunt and that was what got me hooked on the West. But there was one year we went to California to visit Aunt Edith and Uncle Clayton near San Francisco. That was a long, two week stretch of driving. We visited the redwoods, then old friends of my folks in Salem, Oregon. One year we visited Yellowstone. These vacations were rather tame. We never had car trouble, no one broke a leg or got lost, and somehow, my brother and I were well behaved in the back seat. I suppose we had a large supply of comic books, but we did play the alphabet game a lot, as well as car license plate contests. My memory has erased all but the impressions of the mountains and vast open spaces. The West overpowered all else. I was hooked. Flatland Illinois was never the same. It was just a temporary inconvenience.

⌒

On special occasions, most often on a Sunday afternoon, but sometimes after supper, Mom or Dad would make ice cream. Like finicky kids everywhere, I found what should have been a treat, to be something unwelcome. I didn't like homemade ice cream. She would set up the wooden cylinder, the metal motor and paddle, the bag of salt, then mix up the ingredients and turn on the motor. I don't remember how long it took, but Mom, Dad, and Ron stood in anxious anticipation for the magic to result. I usually ate some, but I longed for the commercial variety. There are probably many things all of us would like to go back and change. A big one in my life is that I would savor such treats as homemade ice cream.

July and August evenings were also synonymous with bacon, lettuce and tomato sandwiches. Summer evening meals were nearly always late. They had to await the end of Little League games, so supper was usually after 8 pm. And most evenings they consisted of BLTs, with Dad's huge beefsteak tomatoes fresh out of the garden. Dad had gardened since he was a little kid and his garden was his life. And tomatoes were the mainstay. A typical tomato—which he grew from the seeds he saved from the best tomatoes each summer—was from 2 to 3 pounds. The taste, like the smell of the Hotel Douglas barbershop cologne, is something that will never leave my memory. Not a tasteless grocery store tomato, but a taste that brought on hints of paradise. The bread was lightly toasted and slathered with mayo, the lettuce also out of the garden, and topped with crispy bacon and huge slices of tomato copiously dribbling juice. I could eat a half dozen of them, and usually did. This is a memory that I would not want to go back and change, and I would give my soul to go back and experience one of those BLTs on a hot July or August night. Embellish the BLT feast by sitting out on the front steps later that night watching fireflies. I know what heaven will consist of if I am patient enough to get there.

August nights in Tuscola. I vividly remember the fireflies. I loved watching the fireflies darting and flitting across the lawn, accompanied by the chorus of cicadas and crickets, the unseen orchestra playing their monotonous melodies throughout the night. They turned on their lights at dusk and lit the dark night like lanterns at a party. I never wondered what happened to the fireflies during the day. Some things were accepted. I would catch a firefly in my hands, close my fist carefully, and watch the light between my fingers: magic. Then I would let him loose and watch his brilliant streak as it floated across the lawn, circling and climbing and darting with its companions. After I moved out West, I never again could sit outside on an August night and watch fireflies; they are a mid-western and eastern phenomenon. Once, when I went back to Illinois in mid-summer, I sat outside with my old friend Max and watched fireflies. Fireflies, like home towns, never leave the boy or the man. They are eternal.

EIGHTEEN

Things to Do

In STEREOTYPICAL MOVIE towns, as well as in actual small towns, it seems kids universally complain there is nothing to do. I have never understood this because I imagine kids in bigger towns and cities complain about the same thing. It makes you wonder if it might be the kids themselves.

I never worried about having nothing to do. In the summer, we had Ervin Park: slides, merry-go-rounds, jungle gyms, ball diamonds, swimming pool, and tennis and basketball courts; there were lots of climbable trees, the old bandstand to jump onto and climb to the upstairs veranda, the dilapidated amphitheater, and paved loop roads to bicycle on. The school-yards had much the same. The town was one-mile-square, filled with tree-lined paved streets just made for bicycles. The Strand movie theater had daily shows and matinees on the weekends. The Tastee Freez and later the Dairy Queen were "hang out"spots, as were Mel's and Monical's later on. The Community building had teen-town and other dances for those so inclined. The pool hall was for grown-ups and off-limits to me, although I would occasionally sneak down to see what it was all about. Gus's was always good for a hamburger and phosphate, and the booths were great hang-out spots as well, as long as Gus wasn't busy.

There were few organized activities other than summer Little League, so we were left to function on our own. I think we did quite well, and in those days we had no fear of roaming all day in town, and our parents had no worries either. We knew how to play. Quite often, a basketball carried around town gathered young athletes like a magnet. You could take a tennis racket to the park and usually find someone to play with. More than once in my younger days, a stick and a can or rock attracted enough to play in the streets. Or putting rocks on the railroad tracks across from my house and then knocking them off with thrown rocks; if only I could have hit a baseball as well as I hit those rocks.

Summer thunderstorms were a bonanza, for, in central Illinois, a July cloudburst could easily dump over an inch of rain, which quickly made lakes and streams of the city streets. Who cared if the water was a little muddy? To the dismay of mothers all over town, that attitude carried over to a lack of concern if our bodies ended up more than a little muddy. Besides playing in the erstwhile lakes and ponds, I found intrigue in watching the nightcrawlers surfacing all over the yard gasping for oxygen as their tunnels in the lawn became flooded death traps.

In the winter, free time was limited due to school, shortness of daylight, and cold weather. I did find much entertainment in shoveling the snow off not only our sidewalks but the lawn itself as I built large snow mountains. Sometimes the mound morphed into a fort with walls and tunnels. This geomorphic activity should have been a clue to my parents that I was destined to head for the mountainous West as soon as I had a chance. I had no idea what the neighbors or passers-by thought of this rather odd behavior, but I didn't care. I worked hard and had a visible product to show for it. My parents put up with this since they did get the sidewalk shoveled, not to mention half of the yard. The neighborhood was devoid of kids my age, except for Tommy Martin and I don't ever remember him helping with this mountaineering. His parents probably convinced him he had better things to do.

Tree climbing was optimal due to the variety of large trees in town, but especially in the large white ash tree in front of our house. The park contained a lot of smaller evergreens, which provided a challenge—sharp needles.

I had the misfortune to live in a neighborhood of spinster ladies rather than kids close to my age. Pearl and Grace, two older sisters, lived across the alley and they greatly disliked those Colwell kids. Stella lived next door and was friendly to us until I became old enough to toss baseballs onto her roof. Until he moved across town, Jimmy Allison, my age and schoolmate, would join me in taking a roll of caps from our cap guns and pound them with a hammer on the sidewalk in front of Pearl and Grace's house. Is it any wonder they called the cops one Halloween when someone threw their garbage cans into their yard? My brother vividly remembers this since he was blamed, knowing full well it was probably Steve Allison and Godfrey Ebright.

Our church would occasionally rent a school bus and take a bunch of kids plus chaperones to Mattoon for roller skating. There was a skating rink on the edge of town and we would pile out of the bus, rent skates, and wobble around the rink. Some of us were good, others pretty bad. I don't remember where I was on that scale, but I do remember falling quite a bit. I think I was too young to be worried about impressing any girls. We skated to music and I remember the man who ran the rink. I can still see his face as he rather nonchalantly skated round and round all night long. One trip to Mattoon was on a rainy night and I was sitting in the front of the bus. It was raining so hard, it was hard to see the road and I made some cute comment about praying (this was a church group, remember?). I think I was seriously scared but the bus driver wasn't worried.

Besides the Strand Theater, which had a long and varied history by itself, there was the drive-in west of town. The sole purpose of this was to provide a place for boys to take their girls and make out in the car. Since I didn't date very much, that left me out. However, get a few guys together and you inevitably had the situation of three boys stuffed in the trunk while one drove the car in and paid for just one. Once parked, usually along the edge or some back corner, then the driver got out—after delaying long enough to panic the guys inside— and opened the trunk. I only remember one time going to the drive-in. My brother took me, although I was not impressed by the title of the unknown movie. It was a double feature—they almost always were—and the main feature was an unknown named Sean Connery starring in a movie called *Dr. No*. I did enjoy the movie, especially Ursula Andress.

As we got old enough to work at summer jobs, many of the boys went to work in the cornfields, detasseling. This involved sitting on a mechanical contraption that was driven through the cornfields while the guys picked off the tassels. DeKalb, Pioneer, and other corn producers grew hybrid corn and this involved not letting mother nature take her course. The tassels were pulled off and the ears were fertilized some other way from another plant. It was hard and boring work and I stayed away from it due to my hay fever. Being out among the corn plants like that would have put me in bed sneezing for a month. So I found other ways to make money.

My earliest recollection of employing the work ethic that surrounded us was helping my folks walk the harvested corn-fields in the autumn, picking up ears of seed corn that had been missed by the harvest, and taking the corn to the elevator for cash. This was in the days when the harvest was so inefficient that bushels of corn were left on the ground, and growers allowed this followup harvesting. We walked the fields with large gunny sacks and picked up ears. It was backbreaking work and for an 8 or 10-year-old, unbelievably boring.

The surrounding farms did offer other employment if you looked hard enough and were willing to work. One summer in high school, my brother and I found a job pulling weeds out of a soybean field. This was before the use of chemicals became commonplace. Bob Williamson hired us to walk the quarter-mile-long fields of beans, pulling pigweed, volunteer corn, and other weeds. We used a hoe for most of this, which was backbreaking after about the first row. One day, I wanted to do something else later in the morning, so I got up early, drove out to the field, and did my share of the work from 6 am to 9 or 10. That was my first real understanding of Illinois humidity. A thick dew covered all the plants, which usually had dried by the time we got to the field around 8 or 9. I became sopping wet as I walked through the bean rows, which were about two feet high; I didn't do that again.

My first "regular" job was scorekeeper, announcer, and groundskeeper for Little League in Ervin Park. My brother held this position before me, and as I outgrew my pathetic ball-playing days, I inherited the position. The pay wasn't great, but it was steady for a few weeks every summer. A lot of responsibility for a 13-year-old, but I enjoyed it. I continued my brother's tradition of keeping a large art book filled with stats: every player's offensive and defensive statistic of his whole year, capped by a year-end summary on an index card, complete with a small colored logo of the team. The players loved it. When I cleaned out my parents' house after their deaths, I found the large book under a bed and I donated it to the Douglas County Museum. I don't know if any 70-year-old former Little Leaguer today knows it is there but his baseball history is still there for anyone to see.

Somewhere in my late grade school years, I became a paperboy for the *Champaign News-Gazette*. My route consisted of approximately four town streets with about 60 customers. It was an afternoon paper (except Sunday mornings), and the bundle of newspapers was delivered to my front step mid-afternoon. I would come home from school, fold and rubber band the papers, load them in the large basket of my Schwinn bicycle and start pedaling and throwing. I was conscientious about making sure the paper landed on the porch or steps. I don't ever remember having a paper land on a roof, but once in a while, it did land in a bush, which I then had to retrieve and place correctly. There were a few customers who wanted the paper put behind the door or in a mailbox. Some of them paid me extra, a few didn't, but I didn't care. The only challenge was on a Thursday when the paper was extra thick with ads and my bicycle was front heavy. I lost the whole load on many occasions when I had to park the bike early in my route to retrieve an errant throw.

Saturday was collection day. Everyone paid weekly and in cash. A paper route not only gave responsibility, but it also helped with bookkeeping and math. I had a hardbound collection book with a sheet of thick poster paper with perforated payment tabs for each customer. Some people left money in a jar hidden on the porch, some I had to find at home to be handed the money. Quite often a customer was not at home and I had to make repeat efforts, often going onto Monday or later. I don't remember anyone paying the paper directly, by year, month, or week; I was the only contact.

When I had my bag full of coins, occasionally a few bills (which required the accurate making of change), I rode downtown to the Tuscola National Bank on the corner of Sale and Main, handed my money over, got a money order, and mailed it to the newspaper. Of course, I first had to peruse all the coins to find any dates and mint marks I needed for my coin collection. Sometimes I would find a rare gem and almost always

I would find one coin I needed. Many very good things have been lost over time, one of which is the old fashioned paperboy. It taught responsibility as well as math, accounting, banking, and people skills.

I had a few tough customers, but most were very friendly, and more than a few treated me well at Christmas. I can still remember many of my customers and where they lived. Wib Hoel called me Little Joe and always commented to my dad how good I was. I delivered to the Highway Patrolman, a couple of former and future teachers, even Stella Cullison, our next-door neighbor who had hated that ten-year-old neighbor kid a few years earlier. Orville Proffitt (his son Red owned the Oldsmobile dealership) had coon dogs that lived in a pen behind the house and barked all the time. Mr. Fox was 90 years old and probably knew many Civil War soldiers in his youth. Several I rarely saw since they left money out in a jar on the porch. I don't remember getting any complaints and only once or twice did a customer call to say they didn't get their paper. I was thorough and conscientious. Small town paperboys are a thing of the past, at least ones who rode a bicycle and collected money every week.

※

Since my mother worked at the Ben Franklin store downtown, I was hired as a stock boy. I particularly enjoyed the record section where they sold 45s and long-play albums. I always looked for the new top 40 charts every week from WLS radio in Chicago, and I was able to purchase a fine collection of Kingston Trio, Brothers Four, Limelighters, and other folk groups.

When Don Couch built his new Four Seasons store on Route 36, Ben Franklin brought in Mr. Vincent as manager. He advertised for two high school boys to help set up the new store. Since I was familiar with the store, I got the job along with Roy Davis. We set up shelves, unloaded trucks, and got the store up and running.

My mother and I soon went to work at Four Seasons. I enjoyed the new digs as a stockboy, soon advancing to an actual salesman at times. One day I was asked to go on an errand downtown. Marge told me to take her car since I didn't have my own. It was a stick shift, which I had never driven before. She said it was easy. That was how I learned to drive a manual transmission. I left the parking lot fine, but when I got to my destination and had to stop, I bounced like a jackrabbit until I stalled. But by the time I got back to the store, I could drive a manual. Barely. I also drove Don's Lincoln Continental Town Car to run errands for Don; that was luxury. Four Seasons was popular for miles around and the store was quite upscale for a town like Tuscola.

⤳

I was not social and preferred to do things by myself most of the time. I didn't run with a group or belong to a social clique, nor did I date much, but I always found something to do in this quiet little town of Tuscola. When the weather forced me inside, I read a lot. My books from the Weekly Reader Book Club took up several shelves of my bookcase, and I eventually advanced to books in my dad's collection and from the library.

The cry of "there is nothing to do" indicates a lack of imagination or curiosity by those who say it. There was always something to do, even for a ten-year-old.

NINETEEN

MUSIC OF THE PRAIRIES

DURING THE 1950s and early 1960s, Carl Kohrt was the music man of Tuscola. Mr. Kohrt taught band in the Tuscola schools and I was first introduced to him as I struggled with the cornet in the 7th grade. I don't know if learning to play an instrument was my idea but most likely not; I could blame it on my mother. My first music lessons were in the new North Ward (the old high school). There was a music room tucked away in those brick confines, isolated, of course, from nearby classrooms and hopefully well insulated.

Mr. Kohrt was amazingly talented. He could in one class graciously take my cornet and demonstrate how to tongue, while the next hour take Carol Schrodt's clarinet and chew the reed while easing out a semi-pleasant sound; then the next hour, help Doug Carnine whack the rims of his snare drum. I'm sure he was a demon on the piano, too. This talent made a big impression on a teenager intimidated by one measly instrument. I would rank this alongside the talent required of, say, baseball superstars Stan Musial and Mickey Mantle, or all-around heroes like Roy Rogers.

I lacked talent but was supposed to obtain it by practicing. This was the real torture of the whole experience—homework. In an obviously untrusting move, he had us actually mark down our homework practice and have our parents sign it, attesting to the fact we really did spend that time practicing. I usually went to my dad. He didn't question that my 35 minutes was marked as 1 hour. I'm sure it seemed even longer to him. Mom usually said something to the effect that it didn't seem like an hour. Go figure. Dad probably would have paid me to lie even more, but he was too honest to conspire in such a blatant distortion of the truth; maybe if I'd left my bedroom door open instead of closed.

I do know that by the 8th grade, we played together as a band before class in the mornings. It made me feel important, even if I was mediocre. This was all preparatory, though, to the major league—high school band. This included the marching band, and it meant uniforms: Old Gold and Black, our school colors. Black pants with that slick gold stripe down the side, a big black coat with the gold strings and ropes including brass buttons, and the hat! Really cool to a shy freshman.

I was third level cornet. Tom McDaniel was first cornet and he was good. Dave Lecher was third like me. Gary Forrester was up there with Tom. My first couple of years are faded in my memory, lost in the insecurity of a shy freshman groping his way through high school and the seniors and juniors. Mr. Kohrt stood up there and waved his baton—there was no distinction in his mind between seniors and juniors or anyone else—and helped us all fine-tune our talents.

An annual event was Band Contest. The whole band boarded a bus and traveled to exotic places like Gibson City, Mahomet, Monticello, or other parts unknown to car-less freshmen. We would play a couple of pieces, then wander around town all day while the separate duets, trios, and individual recitals were held. I don't recall any of the actual performances; my main memory is going into a grocery store and buying a can of sardines for lunch, then being razzed for smelly fingers the rest of the day. This was before such luxuries as a McDonald's or other fast-food restaurants. Overall, a genuine adventure—a bunch of teens turned loose in a strange town. Of course, we had chaperones, but somehow we still roamed the streets. No one got into trouble, though some surely looked for it. But remember, this was the early

1960s in mid-state Illinois. "Trouble" certainly had a different definition than today.

We played the *Music Man* in front of the old Strand Theater to advertise the newly released movie, then we entered marching to get a free showing. Quite dramatic, though in retrospect, a little commercial. No matter—a free movie is a free movie.

Springtime brought not only the end of school but Decoration Day ceremonies at the cemetery, including a parade. The TCHS band was asked to march in it and the elite were picked to do honorable duty. Usually, this was after school was out for the year and an honor since we didn't have to be there. Tom McDaniel or Gary Forrester would sneak off unnoticed behind the mausoleum. We would play taps and Tom or Gary would play the echo. Now that is real pressure: solo! A third cornet would never be allowed to solo—we would screw up under that kind of pressure.

When I played in the marching band, I didn't screw up very much. The reason had nothing to do with my talent. I simply didn't play much while I marched. I faked it. We are all good at something. I was good at faking. I knew the songs and I fingered the horn quite well. I just didn't blow into the mouthpiece. Others did it, but it was hard for me! Remember those car commercials where the smooth ride allowed a glass of champagne to look as if was standing still while the car was moving? Well, I didn't have a very good suspension and my glass was bouncing all over the place. Besides, there were plenty of others to make the music. I had to concentrate on keeping in step in a straight line. What would be more embarrassing—being out of step and causing a crooked line, or not adding one voice to dozens of others? Easy choice for me—I stayed in step. Well, there could be disagreement over that one, too. Come to think of it, why was I there at all?

Because it was either band or chorus; the plot by school officials to instill some sort of art or culture in us was effective. I certainly didn't want to sing. Flashbacks of my humiliating episode in 6th grade with Mrs. VanVoorhis , the grade school music teacher, trying to get me to sing still haunted me. That was during the time I had a crush on Glenda Cook. We had to sing solo for Mrs. VanVoorhis so she could figure out where our vocal talent could best be used. I had the nightmare of singing my solo piece when Glenda was in the room listening along with a dozen others. My croaking off-key would have sent frogs running for cover. Certainly no impressing Glenda that day. So I opted for band, not chorus.

I endured, and the big question that still looms is: "was Mr. Kohrt aware of my shenanigans?" Not sure about that one. He knew I was capable. If he knew, then he also knew it was pointless to make an issue of it. This turns into a Nixonian dilemma; if he knew, why didn't he do something; if he didn't know, he should have. I've never been a teacher, so I don't know all the philosophy and strategies involved, but I'm sure there comes a point when life is so much easier just letting things be, even if they aren't quite as you want them. At some point, junior or senior year, Mr. Kohrt asked me if I wanted to play baritone instead of cornet. I could be one of only three baritone players versus one of a dozen cornet players. This put me on the spot. But I went for it: Richard Lindsey, me, and someone else whose name I don't remember.

For a couple of years, Gary Forrester ruled as cornet section tyrant. He intimidated me for two reasons. He was a year ahead of me and he was a really good horn player. Gary was a cutup and actually kind of an obnoxious bully. He reveled in putting Junior Mints on the seat of unsuspecting neighbors, or the ultimate—in the mouthpiece of other horn players' instruments. Gary was socially corrupt, but it kept us all giggling, probably to the dismay of Mr. Kohrt, who may not have known what was going on and probably didn't want to know.

And there were tragedies. I will always remember where I was on the day President Kennedy was shot. We were in the cafeteria during band study hall—we had one day a week break from playing. Mr. Kohrt somberly stated there was an announcement from Mr. Robertson the principal. He announced the news as we all sat around the tables listening. Mr. Kohrt was a rock of support as we absorbed the shock. It was sobering. Few events I remember vividly. That one, I—along with millions of others—will take to the grave: band study hall with Mr. Kohrt, on November 22, 1963, in the cafeteria at Tuscola High School.

And who can forget the milk? Or foam. Or whatever it was that hung at the edge of his mouth. He always had that white at the corners of his mouth. We all have our little foibles. That was his, whatever it was. Probably the result of his intense concentration. Or maybe ground up enamel from gritting his teeth trying to produce something from the collection of adolescents.

All in all, Mr. Kohrt was a Tuscola legend. He was good and he inspired many kids. He kept with it for many years. And the Tuscola Band during his reign was the envy of central Illinois. He left Tuscola soon after I graduated. I know the Band could never have been the same. Despite my pranks, I do appreciate him and regret not trying harder than I did. That has to be a strong compliment, and to the spirit of Mr. Kohrt, I thank you, and may you always wave your baton in pride.

TWENTY

ALL HALLOWS EVE

We SIMPLY KNEW it as Halloween, although technically, it was "All Hallows Eve." Who knew what a hallow was? The tradition went back centuries to the ancient Celtic festival of Samhain, which was converted to All Saints Day by one of the Pope Gregorys. A 10-year-old obviously cared nothing for why we celebrated this day. It meant one thing: trick or treating. It was about candy, not a religious or historic festival. Ten-year-olds can easily filter through things to simplify the true meanings.

I was probably the only kid who donned his costume for two nights in a row. Picking the costume and wearing it was too much work to limit it to a one night stand. People were kind, although probably thinking what is this kid doing out on the night before Halloween? I could say I enjoyed pretending to be a bum or pirate, but it was simple greed for candy.

In Tuscola of the late 1950s we roamed the streets after dark by ourselves, in pairs, or threes. We were not afraid of the dark and the streets were safe enough. We trusted our neighbors. And we didn't worry about needles in candy; the treats were safe, though not all that healthy.

There was an occasional TP-ing of someone's yard, usually done by a high school freshman or sophomore but rarely did we do a trick on anyone who was too stingy with candy. I knew to avoid the houses of curmudgeons who might close the door on me. Why waste my time? I knew who was generous.

Back then, you didn't go to a store to buy a costume. We

made our own, or at least I did. An old bum was a favorite, cobbled from my dad's old work clothes, weathered floppy hat and a mysterious cigar, still in cellophane wrapping which for some reason was tucked away in the buffet drawer in the dining room. I didn't take the cellophane off but stuck it between my teeth, wrapper and all. I couldn't imagine anyone actually smoking this smelly thing.

We displayed our costumes at school, then there was a downtown parade in the afternoon. After wolfing down a hurried supper, I hit the streets. I don't think we emphasized the macabre or spooky—we liked princesses, bums, pirates, and simple things we made ourselves. I can't remember anything like a zombie or skeleton, but I was focused on one thing—the candy.

Although I won awards for my bum outfit in 1957 and maybe another year, my most embarrassing costume was a dress and a wig. Where I got the wig, I had no idea. There was a party next door at the Keigleys—three sisters—and I was the only boy. I pretended to be some female type, young and perky, but not being around girls that much, I was not familiar with the female mode of dress. I didn't know what to wear under the dress! I wore only underpants and realized disaster loomed as I sat cross-legged. Yes, boys are different from girls.

We were invited to decorate downtown windows, so we paired-up and painted pumpkins and skeletons and spooky things. I remember vividly the Halloween of 1960. After carefully painting trees and pumpkins on the windows of the Five and Dime store, I think it was with Donna Ard that I ran the two blocks to the railroad station on the west end of town to greet the train carrying Richard Nixon on his whistlestop election tour. I was a big Nixon fan, but primarily because I had a big crush on his daughter Julie.

Halloween itself came and went, but the autumn days linger in my mind. The smoke rose and wafted in the light breeze from burning maple leaves raked and piled deep, usually a great place to run and jump in before they were burned. There was a crisp hint of the coming winter, especially as we roamed the streets after dark, but days still were mild. Late October had worn the rough edges of the new school year just enough to where we were becoming comfortable with new teachers and some new friends. Maybe that was the attraction of the costumes. We could be free from ourselves, hidden in anonymity. I could not tell you what we were being taught in fifth or sixth or seventh grade the last day of October in 1960 Tuscola. But I vividly remember what I wore and even what kind of goodies I filled my grocery bag with. And of course that historic glimpse of Nixon.

The times were innocent, we say now, 60 years later. We saw them as daring as we stepped out of character and roamed the dark streets free of worry. Now we fear needles and poison and gangs who destroy the fun we were familiar with. Kids must be escorted by adults, a few with guns hidden in bags, while police prowl. I doubt if today's kids know what an all saint is. Would a ten-year-old now understand if I told them?

The autumn nights still hint of the chill yet to come. Piles of leaves still smolder in the streets, but only if it is a burn day. We need the escape now more than ever. Will we ever be able to safely roam after dark dressed like bums and pirates? I also wonder: what did my folks do with the cellophane-wrapped cigar?

TWENTY-ONE

CHRISTMAS

CHRISTMAS CAN BE seen as two holidays: the commercial gift-giving time of year when Santa visits and children await the magic day with anticipation; and the other is the true meaning of a person long ago and what he stands for. Kids wait for the first. Adults play up the Santa part but seriously look for more of the latter. What happens when we are no longer kids? If I focus on the Santa part, it does not mean what it did when I was eight years old. And not having children of my own, I didn't live it through the eyes of offspring. The young eyes keep the sparkle of anticipation; no young eyes, no sparkle. We need to remember the true meaning.

As a child, the entire world is magic—but Christmas! That day I waited all year for contains memories dearer than time itself. I remember Christmas past in a thousand ways, all magical. The annual church play and all the music seemed to last for weeks; this was before the commercial hoopla and store decorations started around Labor Day. The school activities and decorations we made in homeroom art and music classes heightened our anticipation. Who can forget making earrings out of round Christmas mints, white with red stripes? My mom thought them pretty, but I don't remember her ever wearing them. In town, we searched for and found the perfect tree in one of several lots; at home, we dug out boxes of decorations and sat around the card table to write dozens of Christmas cards. The presents were often difficult to select. It was easy for me to make a long list for myself, but what could I get Mother?

It often resulted in a new cookie sheet or the inevitable Oil of Olay facial lotion. Another tie for Dad? Maybe batteries for his coon hunting flashlight?

It didn't always snow before or even on Christmas day, but I would wait anxiously for Santa driving his sleigh through dancing snowflakes. Why couldn't I ever hear those noisy reindeer? As with most kids, I did believe in Santa. How could I question my parents who so vividly described this jolly old man? Until one morning a couple of weeks before the big day—while snooping in my parents' closet—I discovered many wrapped packages with the tag "to Joe, from Santa." My heart and hopes were devastated. Christmas, or at least Santa, was never the same.

Ornaments were family heirlooms and didn't change from year-to-year. The boxes were time-worn, and we handled them with care. Multicolored glass balls—plastic was not in vogue then—had their place high or low on the tree. Tinsel was re-used every year, so it was carefully draped over branches, then just as carefully repacked string by string. Long tubes were filled with bubbly, colored liquid—no doubt long ago deemed a fire hazard and banned. They were all unpacked with glee and anticipation, later put away with dejection and the long wait of another year. The tree that brightened the living room along with our spirits was tossed in the alley, used up along with wrapping paper and broken toys.

Although Santa and presents and trees and decorations were center stage, I did realize the real meaning of Christmas. On the way to Christmas Eve service at church, I remember walking to our garage, two houses down from our house on one cold and snowy Christmas Eve. I looked up at the December sky, wondering if this was the same sky the baby in the manger saw. We drove to church to listen to the familiar carols and hymns. That night, I felt the significance and somberness of the true meaning. Were we all forgetting that, in the focus on Santa and reindeer feet?

The magnificent auditorium of the new North Ward held all the students as we had our play and songfest. We boys thrilled in singing "We Three Kings of Orient Are Smoking our Exploding Cigar. Bam. We Two Kings...Silent Night." Did any of us know the real words?

I have no idea when it started, but our family tradition was always there—bundling up and jumping in the Plymouth to drive around town looking at lights. Who had the best displays? I know Denny Dietrich, electrician and fire chief, usually wowed us—his large house was covered in lights, the old fashioned kind well before the LED or blinking assemblies of icicles and draping strings of lights. In later years, I've found each town I lived in or near had a Denny Dietrich or two or three, who went all out with holiday decorations.

Time passed and Christmas meant travel home from college a half continent away. A vacation for me, a struggle to buy gifts, visit old friends, and a futile attempt to show the excitement I had lost. The Santa Christmas was indeed for kids. Now, Mom would fuss because vandals had stolen her outdoor decorations. "What is life coming to?" she would complain. She vowed she wouldn't put out decorations the next year. Her childhood was further away than mine. My childhood had kept her excitement. No longer. I vividly remember her stories. When she was a young girl, an orange from far off Florida was the most exciting gift possible. She was poor, from a large family and an orange was an extravagant and special gift. Would an orange please me?

Times change. The past grows up. The Santa part of Christmas is in my past. Christmas defined my childhood. When the childhood is lost, so is the grandeur of the Santa Christmas. Was it a lie to make us believe in Santa? I felt then, but so much more so now, we have lost the spirit, the meaning. Retailers decorate in October or even September; it is all about selling, the pressure to buy. Do we have to lose the excitement? Do we have to grow up? Now, in my later years, I look up at the December sky with more questions than answers.

And, now, I also celebrate the solstice. It is even more ancient than Christmas. The early Christians built on the ancient pagan celebration. We expand the stories, build new ones, add music, add magic. Would I go back if I could? What would I want to see or hear or touch? A tree, a bubbling ornament, a mother's story of an orange when she was as young as me? I think I might opt for the anticipation. The thrill of all the magic of the season: music, lights, decorations, family. It rests now entirely in my memory, magnified and enhanced.

TWENTY-TWO

EARLY DAYS OF TELEVISION

As AN EARLY Baby Boomer, I came along at the perfect time. I vaguely remember not having a television, the new invention coming of age about the same time I did. A few years older, like my brother, and I would have had to settle for the good old days of radio. A few years later, and TV would have been an established and permanent fixture.

I remember a few times my family walked several houses down the alley to the Allison's to watch TV. Lee had a radio and TV shop, and helped usher television into Tuscola homes in the early 1950s. I remember watching wrestling, roller derby, and maybe Oral Roberts, but not much else. Maybe there was not much else on in those early days.

My brother was about the same age as Steve Allison, and I was Jimmy's classmate. We played a lot when they were neighbors, but a few years later, Lee moved his store out to Highway 36 and the family lived upstairs above the store. By then, television was no longer new and we all had TVs. No color of course, but the cabinet with the TV was a major piece of furniture in the living room, hooked to an antenna like those springing up on roofs across town.

After we bought our own TV in the early 1950s, I spent many Saturdays lying on the floor glued to the adventures of *Rin Tin Tin, Sky King, Roy Rogers, and The Lone Ranger. Captain Kangaroo* served the function a later generation enjoyed with

Sesame Street; who can forget Mr. Greenjeans and the rabbit? Did the rabbit have a name? And after school was spent with the *Mickey Mouse Club*—Annette, Bobby, Darlene, and Cubby. How many others can you remember?

Sunday suppertime was spent in our house watching *Lassie*, as we ate hot dogs and beans, or those new-fangled TV dinners—Salisbury steak or fried chicken, mashed potatoes, green beans and cherry desert. Tommy Rettig played Jeff, with Jan Clayton playing Ellen. And Gramps was there to provide both fatherly and grandfatherly advice and wisdom. I think they lost the best part of *Lassie* when Jeff was replaced by Timmy, although I did like June Lockhart as his mother. But the best part came when Lassie went to live with U.S. Forest Service Ranger Corey Stuart, played by Robert Bray. Towards the end, Lassie moved over to the National Park Service but this was about the time I moved West to try and become part of the Park Service myself, with my own Lassie. Much later in life, when working with the U.S. Forest Service in Nevada City, California, I worked with Ted Gregg, the Forest Recreation Staff Officer; early in his career he had served as the Forest Service liaison with the TV producers of *Lassie*. When I heard about Robert Bray's death and told Ted as I passed him in the hall at work one day, he said that assignment was the highlight of his Forest Service career.

Saturday evenings were spent watching *Gunsmoke*, Sundays with *Red Skelton* (or was it *Jack Benny*?). What days featured Jackie Gleason and the *Honeymooners*, *Dragnet*, *Have Gun Will Travel*, *Father Knows Best*, *Rawhide*, *Andy Griffith*, *Leave it to Beaver*, *The Twilight Zone*, *I Love Lucy*? Saturday afternoons were spent in rapt attention to Pee Wee Reese announcing the *Baseball Game of the Week*, with color commentary by Dizzy Dean singing about the *Wabash Cannonball*.

Those early days of TV ushered in a new era, replacing the classic radio shows of an earlier time. Many of the plots were new and new stars entered our lives. We could now see them instead of just hear them. Some stars came over from the big screen movies, but new opportunities and careers added many new names to stardom. Clint Eastwood started out as Rowdy Yates. Johnnie Carson started out with a short-lived game show called *Who Do You Trust?*, with new sidekick Ed McMahon, and soon replaced Jack Paar and created classic late-night TV.

As a male, I easily identified with not only the youth shows, such as *Sky King, Lassie,* and *Roy Rogers,* but the night time adult shows as well. Did girls enjoy *Gunsmoke, Have Gun Will Travel, Superman, Father Knows Best?* Why wasn't there a *Mother Knows Best?* Usually, mothers did know best. TV programming then—and still to a lesser degree today—is oriented to men. Who are the women heroes or heroines? *That Girl* and others like it came later. In the '50s and early '60s, it was still a male world.

At my house, we were mostly entertained by the CBS network. We watched WCIA in Champaign, and occasionally WAND in Decatur, the ABC affiliate. We could not get NBC, since the only station in the early days was in Springfield and the reception was snowy. Thus, I missed out on the early NBC shows such as *Bonanza* and *Wagon Train.*

Wednesday nights featured the *Armstrong Circle Theater* hosted by Douglas Edwards, a documentary series that attracted my curiosity, but it was overruled at my house by the Wednesday night fights. My uncle, either George or John, would come to the house and he and Dad watched in rapt attention as boxers knocked the stuffing out of one another—while I waited for commercials so I could grab a minute or two of something I considered much more productive—then back to the fights. We did not own two TVs, nor did very many people I knew. One big set in the living room was it.

CBS *Evening News* originally was a 15-minute broadcast by Douglas Edwards, eventually replaced by "Uncle Walter" as the news expanded to a full 30 minutes, and Cronkite was on his way to TV fame. We trusted Uncle Walter to tell us "That's the way it is."

I think back to all the time I spent in front of the TV and wonder what could have been if I had read or studied instead. But that seemed to be the way we spent our time. I chose a career in part because of *Lassie*. What would have happened if I had envied the profession of Rowdy Yates and become a cowboy? Or become a lawman because of *Have Gun Will Travel* or *Andy Griffith*? Or whatever Jim on *Father Knows Best* was, or Ozzie was on *Ozzie and Harriet*? And what did the father do on *Leave it to Beaver*? Would it have made a difference to me?

What does it mean that I cannot remember a single instance of my sitting in first grade or fifth or seventh, but I can remember some of the episodes of *Father Knows Best* or *Leave it to Beaver* or *Lassie*? I remember one Sunday night lying on the living room sofa sick as a dog from a cold or the flu, listening to the *Jack Benny Show* on TV. I distinctly remember the Phillips 66 gasoline commercial "No matter how you look at it, Phillips gasoline..." and I would always comment, "You look at it upside down and it is 99." But I don't remember anything about math in Mrs. McDaniel's sixth grade.

I have said that memory tells you what is important. Did the early TV shows pound into my brain seriously important themes of life? Although some of the conversations by Ozzie or Matt Dillon or Superman may seem trite today, maybe they were telling me the things I was supposed to learn in church and Sunday School.

What we called educational TV, later to become PBS, was not popular, but I did watch *That Was The Week That Was*—TW3—hosted by David Frost, a biting satire of current events. And I remember that the mothers in the sitcoms seemed to be wiser than the often bumbling fathers. Jackie Gleason in *The Honeymooners* was a pompous jackass, but didn't Audrey Meadows as his wife Alice always bring a healthy portion of intelligence into the picture? I like to think I was not wasting my time with these programs, but absorbed healthy themes of life.

PART III

&

MEANINGS

Is there significance to my fascination with old brick school buildings that no longer exist? There must be a connection with something gone, never to return—like that October day in 1959, and the entire 9 months in Mrs. McDaniel's 6th grade. Like my entire childhood in a place called Tuscola, Illinois.

What was it all about? You stand in familiar places that stretch the cobwebs of your memory. You grew up and you grew old. Wrinkles and white hair replaced the laughter and play of youth. Tears mix with smiles as we see family and friends leave us. But you think back and this is what made your life what it is. And you wonder what lies ahead.

Whether we stay in our hometown for the rest of our lives, or whether we move half a world away, we can always go home. In our memories, we can visit old friends, family, and the old streets and houses of our hometown.

After a lifetime, you can reflect on many things. Not only the past, our history of old friends, family, activities, but also on much larger meanings. How did the past affect each of us? How did it shape the rest of our lives? What meanings can we attach to those old times?

TWENTY-THREE

A PLACE THROUGH TIME

I SPENT MY FIRST eighteen years in Tuscola and consider that is where my roots lie—deep in the black, fertile soil. Even though I left as soon as I could—seeking the mountains, valleys, and wide-open space of the West—my hometown is "mine."

It may belong to me, but I realized, as I put together this collection of memories, that it has always belonged to many others over time. And time is something I am rooted in as well as place. Although Tuscola was my home for a short 18 years, I came to realize that I was only one small segment of a long history. By the time I came along, over a century passed since the first settlers occupied the prairie land that had been called home by peoples for ten thousand or more years. The Illini, Kickapoo, Shawnee, Fox, and countless others, roamed this prairie along with bison, mammoth, smilodon, horses, ancient sharks, even pterodactyls and velociraptors. It was prairie, seafloor, swamp, and other landforms that we can only guess at. The land—once located near the equator—moved, rose, fell, was covered by sand and gravel, ice, and ocean in its 4-billion-year history. My 18 years is insignificant in the big picture.

I knew there was coal, oil, and gas in places throughout the area. I also knew there was a layer of limestone underneath that rich black soil. Far underneath everything lies the bedrock, that granite shield that forms the basis of continental North America. But I did not realize that for millions of years this area sank and rose as seas and swamps came and went.

Ancient rivers ran from east to west. I know that the Creta-
ceous Sea that created the Mancos Shale where I now live in
western Colorado was filled with the sands and muds from the
Appalachians. Thus rivers had to flow westerly through what
I came to know as Tuscola and central Illinois.

But advancing and retreating ice sheets up to a mile thick
covered and scraped the former surface clean time and again
for millions of years. The ancestral Mississippi River once
flowed through the center of Illinois, entrenching itself in its
current position only at the end of the last ice age.

Conifer woodlands throughout the area eventually became
a fertile tallgrass prairie where herds of bison could get lost
in the tall grasses. Native peoples then settled what I would
know as Douglas County for thousands of years, living a life
I can never imagine. They were part of the prairie and lived
through cycles of change for millennia.

So when I look back and say this hometown is "mine," I
realize it is not mine and never was. I played a small part in an
epic drama that continues now and far into the future. That
drama is far bigger than any of us, even the "founders" and
"fathers and mothers" of the little town called Tuscola.

That is why we need to know and understand history, not
just about our kind, but all that came before us. Does it matter
that this was once a large swamp that eventually turned into
coal or oil? Does it matter that a shallow sea covered where
my home on E.N. Central Avenue stands? Or that the native
people roamed what are now cornfields and city streets, for
far longer than my ancestors lived here?

It matters to me. As a young boy, looking for seashells in the
graveled parking space in front of our house, I didn't understand why they were there and what that meant. Someone had
told me the seashells were used as money by the native peoples
who used to live here, and I thought that was pretty cool. Many
years later I learned it meant creatures once lived in an ocean
and formed a layer of limestone that was mined and crushed

into gravel to build roads. And the rich black soil was deposited by huge ice sheets plowing the land for hundreds of miles, leaving the most productive soil in the world. And, if we used farming practices that eroded the soil, it would take several future ice ages to once again produce anything as productive.

"My hometown" is mine as well as the home of countless others before me. Children my age once ran through tall grass and sunflowers on a path that later became my street. What I knew as Gus's and Ervin Park were once a shallow ocean where corals and small crustaceans fell through the water to become the limestone that lays under my town. It becomes my responsibility now to honor that history. And "my town" will become history to a future unknowable to me.

TWENTY-FOUR

THE DIVERSITY OF CHANGE

I MOVED WEST IN 1965 and have returned to Tuscola only for occasional visits. Since my father died in 2002, I have not been back at all. During visits between 1965 and 2002, I saw significant changes to the town. Of course, the streets remained the same, most buildings stayed the same, although some burned down, some were torn down, and new ones were built. People moved away from, or to, the area, many passed on, but the overall ambiance remained: a small town and community surrounded by fields of corn and soybeans.

But, being trained as a wildlife biologist and ecologist, I know that nothing stays the same. Habitats change, the land itself changes, new animals and plants come and go. The same with Tuscola. I also know that change brings diversity and diversity is the engine of life. And of towns.

I remember several houses when I lived in Tuscola that were abandoned, or at least looked abandoned—unpainted, with weeds and vines growing in wild profusion. What I called weeds were partially the original inhabitants of the former prairie—wildflowers and grasses trying to reclaim their former wildness. When a building or house was torn down, if it weren't rebuilt immediately, that diversity of life made valiant efforts to return. Diversity did go the other way. A natural area could be bulldozed and tamed with a building or house, a bluegrass lawn, or a paved parking lot.

I have written about the schools that I knew and attended—now gone—replaced by houses and driveways. The same is happening to the old High School—New North Ward Grade School building. Seen now from aerial photos, you can identify the century-old oval track, visible in the large grass field. The building where generations of students studied and prepared for life is gone; the field where those students played or practiced—will soon be covered with houses and flowerbeds. This will add diversity—more flowers for birds and bees, more trees for squirrels, more people who will grow up or grow old. They will then call this home, and judge the future by what they see and hear from now on. A large open space, room for dogs and kids to run and play, will be gone. The past and memories of a school and generations of students will no longer exist except in our minds. Change will continue to alter Tuscola as it has for over a century.

Is this good or bad? In nature, there is no judgment. Nature is amoral. What is good for some may be bad for others. I have stated many times that the Tuscola I grew up with no longer exists. I am sure previous generations stated the same thing. Today's Tuscola will disappear in another two generations. Something else will replace it since the grandchildren of today's children will see change we cannot even fathom.

We are advised to look to the future. We know the past and judge everything by that. But nature doesn't look at things that way. Nature is change and change is life. I mourn for the past I left behind. It will continue to change. We adapt. We look to the past and think what was. Then we turn around and look to the future and think what might be. There is no present. The future changes into the past. That is the miracle of life. Change brings diversity, new things, new ideas. Without it, we stagnate and perish. Then memories are all that remain.

TWENTY-FIVE

GOING HOME

For NEARLY FORTY years, I was able to go home. Home was the town and the house where I grew up and where my folks lived for 60 years, the same house where they were married in 1934. After Mom passed, Dad lived there by himself for his last eight years. I moved out when I was 18, but home was always there for me to come back to. I had something my classmates who stayed—either in town or the nearby area—didn't have. They couldn't because they never left "home." Only those who leave to start new lives elsewhere and create new "homes" can understand coming back to their original home.

My life would be out West and I think everyone knew it by the time I decided on college my junior year in high school. It may have broken Mom's heart but she knew I didn't belong in Tuscola. Although I didn't belong there permanently, I returned many times over the years and experienced the concept of going home. My first big adventure, after leaving for Idaho and college in September of 1965, was returning via my first airplane flight for Christmas that year: I went home for the first time. It was a strange experience. The house was the same but it looked different. Maybe that's because I was different. I was living on my own, albeit on a long financial leash from the folks. But I could "go home"—I didn't "come" home; and there was a difference. Going home was returning to a place where I no longer belonged. Coming home would have been returning to where I belonged after visiting somewhere else.

In the ensuing years, every time I went home, I noticed a

slight difference, but I still was able to call it home and I always said it was a wonderful gift: I entered a time machine and went back to a childhood and a town that never really changed. Any slight differences were overwhelmed by my memories of what I left. I was excited to be able to go back and see what was part of my past. But after a few days, I was equally excited to return to where my new home was. My time machine had a limit of interest after only a few years of using it.

During college, the adventure of flying overwhelmed other interests. I usually flew from Spokane to Chicago to Champaign. There were variations depending on the weather. Once I flew into Pullman, Washington instead of Spokane. One blizzardy winter, the plane couldn't land in Champaign, so we were bussed to O'Hare, then a confusing, congested, and mad rush to get anything flying west from Chicago. I ended up flying into Portland, where my roommate met me so we could drive to California to meet Katherine at her home. Not long after that, I felt going to Pleasant Hill, California, was going home. After we were married, our trips to Tuscola were more to satisfy parents than to actually go "home."

After college, and a brief stint in the Peace Corps, I stayed with my folks on E.N. Central Avenue, while I looked for a job. But I soon realized I was a fish out of water and hightailed it back West. Home was a place to visit, not to stay for more than a few days. After I started my career, I would go home for visits, bringing my wife and dog. I could still walk the streets but I was becoming a stranger. There were fewer and fewer people who even knew who I was.

I walked downtown and I saw only the buildings and experiences I had when I was a boy of ten. (I could have borrowed a bicycle to see if I could remember the paper route I had for several years.) I passed the empty storefronts and businesses that had housed Jay North Furniture, Cohen's Clothing, Ben Franklin, Mills Drug, the vacant lot that was Grab It Grocery. Across the railroad tracks from 204 E.N. Central, I looked at the vacant building that I remembered as the Armory, then Piggly Wiggly, and changed into Eisner's at some point in my childhood. I remember buying Crane potato chips at Eisner's to get the baseball buttons. I had a good collection of those as well as baseball cards from bubble gum packages. I don't know what happened to the buttons, but the cards stayed with me for decades. Neither Piggly Wiggly nor Eisner's were there any longer except in my mind.

Of course, I spent time walking by the old schools that no longer existed: the old North Ward which disappeared after my first four grades, and the South Ward which was replaced by a housing tract; the old white pine planted in memory of an older school that burned well before my time remained, but after a few more years, the pine disappeared as well. I wandered the streets where I collected leaves for my biology class leaf collection. I remembered where the old Kentucky coffee tree was on south Niles and the silver poplar somewhere near the high school. Ervin Park had a good collection of trees, but I didn't remember any specifics.

You go home to revisit memories and sometimes you see ghosts as well, as I did one late 1990s November day in Ervin Park. I stood on the ball diamonds where I spent summer evenings in a Little League Yankee uniform. I heard the sounds of ten and eleven-year-olds pounding their Stan Musial or Harvey Keen mitts.

I went home even further back in time when I stood at the very north end of the Park and could see the crumbling amphitheater. This was a scene that I had to go into my parents' memories to understand: I was a recent visitor to this home town, which had nearly a century of memories I was not a part of. I inherited much that didn't include me, but I was part of. That's what it means to go home. You can go home to a past you were not a part of, only a continuation of. My town belonged to many people I would never know except in old photos or histories. When I went home, I became one of those ghosts who no longer belonged, at least to the people who had inherited what had once been my very own.

Many of my visits were during the Christmas holidays. Going home meant I could recollect the Christmas church plays where—as a terrified six-year-old—I had to recite a few lines as a shepherd or wise man. I could stand outside on a frosty December night and return to the south side Christian church where we went for midnight services; I remember little else, but seeing that vacant old brick building—abandoned as a church for decades—took me back.

I went home and saw the building that once was the old Jarman Hospital, now converted to apartments. That is where I took my first breath on a spring day so long ago; it meant only what my mother told me. After my mother died, that memory left my existence. I am a Jarman baby—now a shrinking group of old people, soon to be as much a memory as the long-gone buildings in historical photos. Many of my classmates moved to town about the time the big chemical plant came in the early fifties. We thought Petro—later USI— was a big boost. Maybe it was, but I cringe when I think now of its toxic chemicals contaminating our air, soil, and water. The last time I went home, most of the plant was disassembled, with only a few skeletal old buildings of what once was the town's pride and joy.

I could go home and sleep in what was once my brother's downstairs bedroom, and lie awake as the trains rolled through town at 3 a.m., vibrating the windows. I grew up listening to the trains of the Baltimore and Ohio or the Central and Eastern Illinois railroads. I remembered the station down the street, long ago torn down, across from what was the *Tuscola Journal* newspaper. I could no longer stand there and watch the hook on the mail car of a westbound freight catch the mailbag from a hook next to the track. I doubt if there is anyone left alive who worked in the mail car sorting mail as the train carried the news and gossip of our country in all directions.

The last time I went home to visit was in the fall of 2001. My brother wanted me to help him replace the rain gutters along both sides of the old house. He also warned me that Dad was talking about not doing a garden the next summer. This was a red flag since Dad had gardened for ninety years and growing vegetables was a huge part of his life. Even in his 90s, he used a spading fork to turn the entire garden; no rototiller for him. The winters were spent perusing all the seed catalogs. Even talk of not gardening was enough to convince me. However, September 11, 2001, changed things forever. I waited a few weeks until planes could fly again and flew into Indianapolis where my brother met me. We tried to replace the old gutters that were barely attached to rotting eaves and eventually gave up. But the visit was good and when I left a week later, I knew there would be very few more visits; I didn't realize at the time there would be none.

I could go home until that day in 2002 when I drove away from the house at 204 E.N. North Central. It was no longer home. It is hard to describe the feeling to realize you can never again go home. The hometown is still there, as are memories of childhood. Someday, I expect to go home one last time to say a final goodbye. But it will not be "going home" since there is no home. There are memories, buildings, familiar street signs, maybe even an old house where I went home for many years, where I lived and grew up and created memories for over a dozen years. But I can never go home again.

Going home was a trip into the past, a visit to memories and spirits only I could see. Memories can be described but they cannot adequately be experienced except by one person in the history of this earth. That is a powerful thought. On that last visit on some day in the future—my farewell visit—I will ponder that meaning. After that, I will go home to a place even I will not recognize. Where or when that home is, I eagerly await a discovery only I can dream of. Then I will be home forever.

TWENTY-SIX

FIFTY SEASONS OF YESTERDAY

THE CLASS OF 1965 held our 50th reunion in 2015. I chose not to attend. Fifty long years had passed. Fifty summers without seeing or talking to most of my classmates. Fifty long and cold winters without knowing how their lives had turned out. Our Tuscola High School class in 1965 lived and dreamed—together, apart, thinking of worlds yet to come, of lives yet to live. I was a stranger to many in 1965; and I would have still been a stranger as many gathered to relive old times, to remember, reminisce, replay old times and old laughs, tears and memories.

Nola Duensing sent me a photo of those who gathered from miles and years apart. I was a curious observer, and I wondered how they turned out. I looked in surprise at the faces, although I don't know why I was surprised—I had changed, they had changed. Fifty years does things to a face, a mind, a life. Forty-six of the ninety-five pictured in our yearbook faced the camera. A few didn't graduate with us but were connected to Tuscola and our class most of those school years. We had lost about 10 who never made it this far. Life can never be predictable.

I pulled out my copy of the 1965 Tuscolian yearbook, and I looked inside the cover at the two-page photo of our class gathered on the football field, squinting into the sun—mostly smiling or laughing, a few distracted, looking in different directions—intent on that autumn we were seniors, ready to conquer our and others' lives. I compared the faces with those in the 50th reunion photo, although there really was no comparing. We were all young, dreaming of a world we were about to inherit, although I noticed a lot of the guys were not smiling and the girls were hesitant. Actually, I felt a hesitancy in most of us. Our eyes were looking at each other, at the camera, out into an ethereal future we were anticipating, fearing, uncertain. Back then, we were the future, expectations were high, our dreams were unlimited.

What changed? Look at the faces of those young people now turned "old" as if any of us felt 68 to be very old in 2015. They all showed the passage of time, life had happened: disappointments, tragedies, lots of wisdom. The story is as old as the very rocks of this earth. Every generation starts as we did. Hopes and dreams, fears and worry. We play together, learn together, dream together in childhood innocence. Then life moved forward as we were blown by a wind that whirled and scattered. A scattering that cannot be put back together.

Look at the faces. Forty-six of ninety-five came together to share those dreams of long ago, perhaps ignoring what happened for the last fifty years, including the dreams met or unmet, the disappointments, the joys, the tragedies. Some lost children or the loves of their lives, parents mostly gone, children grown and grandchildren growing up. Wisdom is nurtured with age; we take what we were given, smile or frown, brag or shed a tear, but accept that life has happened. Looking at the camera, showing a freshness of youth, or the toll of age, all showing the wisdom that comes with life. Not old people—as some of the current crop of high school seniors might think as we surely did at that long-ago age—but children who grew up and still dream of the past just as we used to dream of our future. Why can't we trade places? Take us back fifty years and let us ride into the future and get a hint of what we are anticipating. Then take us back and let us enjoy what we once enjoyed but have now lost. Is that too much to ask?

JoEllen holds onto Bob, who perhaps is thinking of his Shirley who left him and all of us much too soon. Mike shows his politician's smile, right arm around Joe (who moved away before we graduated but stayed in touch), his left hand on Jim's shoulder, a friend like so many who moved away to continue his life. Mike stayed and became a town leader, a mainstay to the past many of us left. Ron looks truly happy, as does Kathy—one stayed, one left. Does that make any difference? And why do the "girls" look younger than the "boys"?

Doug stands slightly apart, the intellectual giant, who always stood slightly apart. Did he know too much? Jim shows a hint of impishness while both Marie and Pam flash smiles of enthusiasm, as does Linda, a class hero whom we didn't honor enough at the time. Donna has a look of uncertainty, and Linda and Anne have an exuberance of youth. Tim has a look I cannot describe; I think back to our big adventure to Colorado in his old black Ford. He and I shared two weeks, then parted never to see each other again; I think, "what a loss for both of us."

On one end, sitting with the pride of achievement is Max. The success of this gathering was part due to his hard work. Our class historian, he understands the deeper meaning of this get-together. It will be the last for some, but miles and years cannot separate what is joined in memory.

Out of the picture, behind the camera and watching, are many others—the spouses or life partners—who share the stories, but not the same memories. The children and grand-children and those who didn't come, of which I was one, are in the thoughts of some. All of those looking at the camera share some memories and each has memories only they hold. Life took each person and gave them a different story to tell. A different life to remember. But common to all is a place and a time that no longer exists except in the minds of these grown-up kids. Memories we all hold more precious than a roomful of gold. Memories that are us in a time called yesterday, that happened over 50 years ago.

TWENTY-SEVEN

CIRCLING THE SQUARE

TUSCOLA, LIKE MOST towns and their surrounding coun-
try-sides in America, is laid out in geometric squares. Streets
and roads, parking lots, buildings, cornfields, and most other
man-made constructions are linear. The survey system used in
this area generally follows the linear latitudes and longitudes
that Earth is divided into. Sections and townships are the
norms nowadays.

Tuscola is divided by the railroad tracks through town into
a north and south, originally the North Ward and the South
Ward. All streets are due north and south, due east and west. I
lived on East North Central, which paralleled the railroad and
was one block east and south of the central focus of town—Sale
and Main Streets.

Ervin Park connected its due north and south roads with a
perfect rounded corner geometrically connecting the two sides,
although the west road does curve so there is some break in
the straightness. Some of the newer subdivisions broke with
tradition and curve and sway in a much more artistic manner.

However, nature does not know straight lines—except for
such things as quartz crystals and diamond edges. Curves,
circles, arcs, and squiggles are nature's artistry. Look at rivers,
mountain ridges, hills, beaches, forest edges. All curved or
winding. Nature's chaos, especially that amazing thing called
fractals, has beautiful symmetry of curves. Since straight lines
are not natural, a linear world gives a false sense of what is real.

Maybe one reason I left Tuscola long ago was I tired of the

geometry of straightness. I craved rounded corners, circles, the undulating ridgetops, and loops and oxbows of rivers and streams. I also came to realize that straight lines break the flow of nature. The ancestral peoples who lived in the tallgrass prairie that became Douglas County—along with virtually all aboriginal peoples—knew that life itself was about circles and cycles. Native dances, drawings, and structures were circular. Teepees, kivas, cliff dwellings, ceremonial mounds knew few straight lines. The sacred circle was the center of worship, delineating directions such as north, south, up and down. All had meaning and all flowed from a circle.

I think of the medicine wheel or the sacred hoop, common to some Plains tribes. They laid small rocks in a circle, linked by lines of rocks like spokes of a wheel. Used in their spiritual practices, the circle gave symmetry and balance, different colors, totems, and meanings to the four directions. For example, the east meant birth, rebirth, or renewal. It might have been represented by the color yellow or white. North meant death or darkness, represented by the color black or blue. In the spiritual worship around the medicine wheel, some holy men or women also added two more directions—up and down. Down was to Earth Mother, the giver of all life. Gaia Earth we call her now, the living planet that breathes and is alive. They knew that all life was woven together in a web that connected all living as well as non-living things.

To me, the last direction is the most interesting: up, to the heavens—Father Sky, the sun, the moon, the stars, and the great mystery. Ancient peoples didn't know the science that now tells us the universe itself is 13.7 billion years old. That time span is incomprehensible to modern people and would have been even more so to our ancestors. The universe is time and time is infinite, unknowable. It symbolizes the mysteries of life, the origins of all things, the spirits of who we came from, and where we are going to. It was the home of the shamans, the holy people, Manitou, the Great Spirit.

None of this was evident to me in that linear flat world of Douglas County.

The spirits of the natives could expand the horizons of the lives of the common people. Horizons could be expanded in the four directions and the people could travel and discover for themselves the limits of the circle. However, it took the holy people to understand where the horizons could expand up or down. That is where the spirits lived. The circle expanded up or down where we could not travel. Except in our minds. And when we can finally connect with those spirits, our circles become infinite. The horizon becomes the sacred road, a winding path that leads to the great mystery and finally to home. At age 18, unknowingly, I decided I wanted to follow the sacred, curvy road.

Cycles, whether animal, plant, weather, or human emotions, are ups and downs. If graphed by our modern analytical minds, they follow symmetrical curves. Populations of rabbits go up, then crash, followed by lynx or coyote or whoever feeds on them. Forests grow, mature, then die by fire or insect. Meadows or brush fields follow in natural succession, to be later overtaken by trees once again. Fires reduced the prairies of pre-European settlement Tuscola and Douglas County; the gray-black ash fertilized the grasses and flowers, which then encouraged the bison and deer to return after moving past the blackened land.

Circles and cycles are a theme I continually return to as I seek to bring nature back into a modern and scientific linear equation. Straight lines are not natural. We cannot return to the way we once were, but we can understand nature's art and beauty as we navigate straight roads and avenues, build square houses, and look straight into the past or future. That linear mentality is predictable, with a loss of ambiguity. The circular world has mystery and patterned chaos.

We are meant to flow like a wild river or seek high places or meander in curved park paths. We do not lose our way as we wind around. We lose our way when we follow a straight line. Think of that next time we follow a winding road through a forest or along a lakeshore. Circles and cycles allow us to breathe deeply and feel the energy too many of us have lost. We cannot find it along the stark grids of city streets. We do find it under a starry night sky as we look for the curved constellations and the rounded full moon, and we listen to the melodic song of the warbler or the haunting cry of the coyote. Let nature flow in its endless curving path.

TWENTY-EIGHT

THE TUSCOLA MURAL

IN THE YEAR 2000, before returning to Tuscola for a short visit, I had read about the mural at the downtown site of the old Hotel Douglas. I thought it a wonderful idea—using the wall facing the vacant lot for a piece of beautification and historic preservation. We need to keep alive bits and pieces of our past that are so ingloriously being allowed to crumble and disappear. I thought how our future is guided, often mysteriously, by our past. If we lose our past, we lose a lot of what makes us who we are. I thought that the three buildings being honored in the mural were very well chosen to represent old Tuscola. Many young people today have no recollection of these parts of the past. They were certainly part of my past and I remember them and Tuscola fondly. I am as much a part of Tuscola as anyone who walks the streets there today, but anyone under 50 years of age would not know me—or old Tuscola institutions such as Phil White, Freddie Jones, or Myrtle Froman.

So I walked with anticipation up to the corner of Sale and Main on a sunny, cold November morning. Workers were still laying brick for a fancy old-fashioned street clock at the site. The corner was fenced off, but yes, a painted mural now grandly covered the side of the building next door. Traffic of this early 21st century morning continued by, as it had every morning for decades beyond memory. Only the technology had changed—fancy new Lexuses replaced fancy new Edsels, replacing technologically new Model Ts, which had replaced the latest in horse and carriage design. The blue of the November sky remained the same over the years, only slightly hazed over this day by the carbon and nitrogen that used to be in the earth, now in the atmosphere above. The fallen and fading reds and yellows of maple, sweetgum, oak, and sycamore now littered the streets, as tree limbs held their naked arms to the sky, encouraging the first winter snow.

My attention turned to the mural. The artist did a very fine job of painting. I thank her and I thank the town leaders for helping me go back to another time, but unfortunately, I felt a tremendous sense of disappointment in how old Tuscola was depicted. I currently live near a small town in western Colorado, which has no less than a dozen murals adorning sides of downtown buildings. They depict, in detail, scenes of local history—from Utes riding past buffalo herds, recent cattle round-ups, old hardware stores, and a display of historic fruit labels from nearby orchards. Delta tells its story through murals, leaving no doubt of its historical pride, and does so with detail and accuracy.

Not so here, at the northeast corner of Sale and Main; I sighed as I inspected "old Tuscola" on the mural. I would be the first to admit my memory plays tricks on me. I really don't remember exactly how the Strand Theater appeared, nor the *Tuscola Journal*, though I spent hours at each. But they didn't appear like this: a bland, generic stereotype of old buildings that could be anywhere. These were not the *Journal* or Hotel Douglas or Strand Theater I knew. These weren't drawn by someone who lived here, who knew them, who knew what they meant to a town of the mid-20th century, middle-America. The mural tells nothing of the history or life of these institutions, but rather, a fanciful depiction—an almost patronizing attempt—to satisfy a need to reconnect to old times. The mural is not the Tuscola I remembered and certainly wouldn't tell millennial teenagers what I, as a mid-century Boomer-teenager saw or felt. I hate to be negative, but the mural is quite frankly, sterile. It is not alive. Is this what history means to today's generation? Is it something they think important because someone said it should be important? Is it something based on imagination and not reality?

I thought back to the way I looked at history when I was a teenager and younger. I respected it, I was awed by it. I knew real people lived in a real town that no longer existed, but I also knew my mother and father remembered stories of what to me was just a building and names of long-dead people. I was intrigued by all that and I knew it was part of me, part of who I was and where I lived. I may not have known the details, but I listened and tried to learn. If anyone tried to learn about the Strand and the *Journal* and the Hotel Douglas as depicted in this mural, they, unfortunately, start with a blank mind and end with a blank picture.

Well, I thought, what can I offer to bring them to life the way I think they should be? I cannot just breeze into town and criticize someone else for a noble attempt at a good idea. I can't add anything from my hands and a paintbrush, but I can add my thoughts and memories as words for others to read. I am now part of history and I can share what I think important to remember about Tuscola and my time there.

I can tell about the Hotel Douglas and the barbershop run by Paul Roderick and Fred Cooch. Going in there on a Saturday morning and smelling the perfumed hair tonic, seeing the stack of comic books and *Saturday Evening Post* on the tables. The bicycles piled on the sidewalk and Paul or Fred's banter. I can see Freddie Jones walking out the door of his hotel with a big cigar in his mouth and hear the clink of plates in the basement café. This was the center of town and it was the Tuscola version of the big city. A multi-story hotel, strangers coming and going, a real café with connotations to a small boy of fancy far off worlds. I would add those sights and smells and memories. That's what the Hotel was, and a lot more. I didn't see any hint of that on the mural.

I can tell about Phil White and the *Tuscola Journal*. The

Journal, born in the 19th century, was here long before Phil White came to town, but for a generation or two, Phil epitomized what a local paper and a feisty white-haired journalist could do for a small town. Phil pulled no punches and he fought for this town. He was controversial and contrary and opinionated, but he was also sane and courteous. I can smell the ink and newsprint from the backroom printing presses. I hear Phil as he looks over my shoulder as I try to put down words in my duties as a teenaged Sports Editor in the early 1960s. He wanted nothing bland. He jump-started my first article by adding "The Tuscola Warriors got their baptism of fire Friday night." Phil pushed this town and made us think and react. His editorials left no doubt where he thought we should go. He also stirred us up just to be contrary. I remember one time he attacked his newspaper rival and downtown neighbor Bob Hastings, accusing him of not even having a bathroom for his employees to use. Bob responded the next week by printing a photo of him and his staff holding a chamber pot and saying he did too take care of his workers! Phil may have infuriated us at times, but he didn't let us sleep when it came to the town and its future. I almost fell asleep staring at the *Journal* storefront on the mural. It needed Phil White's passion and fire. The fire went out, though, long ago in more ways than one, as raging flames took down the *Journal* building and its past editions. More than paper was destroyed that night.

I can tell about the Strand Theater. I still hear the kids yelling and cheering a long-ago Saturday afternoon as the latest Roy Rogers film came to town. The marquee announced Roy and Dale and Gabby, recently replacing the names of Bogart or Hepburn, Gable, or Wayne or Cooper. The Strand was our true escape to the outside world. It took us from the Blob and aliens of deep space to the closer realities—or imagined realities—of our own Western plains replete with bad guys and heroes; tame romances and fairy tales, from *Cinderella* and *Snow White* to the *Music Man*. The Strand was our theater and it gave us heroes we could be proud of and villains who got their just reward. I look at the mural and see no marquee. No heroes, not even a bag of popcorn.

But the mural held me like a magnet. I kept thinking how disappointed I was that the mural lacked accuracy, lacked detail. Then I realized it <u>was</u> there. The detail, the life I lost long ago was magically hidden. My memory simply paints what I want to see. I realized the *Journal* means one thing to me and something different to someone else. My marquee on the Strand announced John Wayne; to my dad, it announced Chaplin or Garbo. The mural, to those of us who have memories, does paint in the detail, even if we have to sit on the sidewalk across the street on a chilly November morning. Memories are not lost; they are not like blank walls, they are just made of disappearing ink that must be allowed to magically reappear after decades of inattention. They have detail in glorious Technicolor. They can smell like barbershop tonic and theater popcorn. They have sounds like clipping scissors and the boos of ten-year-olds when they see the villain aim a pistol at Roy Rogers. They can feel the sting of rain as a thunderstorm lets loose over the flat Illinois prairie just as the movie ends and the kids stream out the front door. Memories may lose a little accuracy over time, but they can be vivid and alive.

My only regret is this mural can't do that for someone who passes this way only after the flames cooled on the fires that stole the real buildings and real memories. I can guarantee to today's teenagers that they weren't bland, generic buildings. And their inhabitants were not fictional characters. I think I will just lapse back into those buildings and have a chat with Phil about last week's Warrior football game. Or more likely about his theory on what people want to read concerning sports and team spirit, the bonding of young athletes, the pride of a hometown. Or I might go in and tell Paul the barber about my round of collecting for my paper route this morning and that I found a really neat buffalo nickel that I didn't have already in my collection. Maybe I will even go out to the lobby of the Strand and buy a bag of popcorn as the couple on the screen gets a little too romantic and mushy for my ten-year-old taste. Then I will go back and sit down and wait for Roy and Trigger to ride back onto the screen. Then I will saddle up and ride off with them into the sunset.

TWENTY-NINE

LOST IN THE SIXTIES

Doo-Wop OF THE Fifties was our older brothers' and sisters' music. The music of my generation came of age with us in the Sixties. The British music invasion included the Beatles, Chad and Jeremy, Dave Clark Five, Gerry and the Pacemakers, Peter and Gordon, and Tom Jones. We took the music, made it ours, and made the time ours.

Back then, at the point when our lives were starting to change—anticipating the tumultuous second half of the Sixties that lay ahead—life was lived one day at a time. Sometimes good and sometimes not so good, it went fast and it went slow. We were growing up and discovering relationships, adventures, consequences. Childhood was for others, maybe younger brothers and sisters, neighbors, friends. We were driving, dating, working to make gas money, planning for college, marriage, jobs, and whatever came next. None of us knew what to expect. We gave it little thought. We were busy having fun, worrying, learning. We couldn't compare the times with anything else. We were inventing life along with ourselves.

Only after years—stretching into decades, past half a century—can we stop, look back, and think about it all. It only happens once in a life and now we can look through the photo albums, the old yearbooks, the letters, the memories, and compare.

We were lost in the Sixties, coming out of the safety and comfort of the Fifties. Coming out of the safety and comfort of childhood in a quiet town like Tuscola. We began the Sixties, and the turmoil and excitement continued for several more years. In Tuscola, the times were tame. Vietnam was only just beginning. Drugs and even sex had come slow, and touched only a few of us. Dragging South Line and Main and Niles, stopping to see who was at Mel's or the Dairy Queen, eating pizza at Monical's—those were the exciting events each week. We were focused on what was happening within the town boundaries, within the county lines, but seldom further out. The world was out there waiting but we were holding back, waiting for the starting gun.

We watched Mike and Don, Hoot and Jim, Tim and Allen parade in their cool black and gold T jackets. They brought us pride and joy. We watched Anne—a brand new Miss Tuscola— and Shirley twirl the batons, Mary lead the cheers, Linda travel the world as an Olympian. We listened to Jim and Angela lead the music. We were our own heroes and heroines.

The times were alive and we look back now, with squinting eyes and wrinkled faces, watching our grandchildren follow in our footsteps, but they are not ours anymore. Our footsteps were left a long time ago. They are impressed in the sands of time, solidified like dinosaur footprints in sandstone. They still echo and vibrate under a blue sky now lost as it fades through the universe. These children and grandchildren are forming their own memories in their own world, changed beyond recognition from ours. Tuscola, a small town like thousands of others, formed us, guided us, developed children into adults, and threw us upwards and outwards—as we stayed or left—and created new lives. We are who we are because of what Tuscola was and because of those before us who did what we did but in a slightly different way. We are different from previous and future generations, yet we are the same.

We are part of a generation that later fought the system and led the charge to add dignity and equality to what we feared to be a corrupt system, or at least a system veering astray. Our early heroes, such as stalwart fictional characters

Roy Rogers, Sky King, Batman, and Lassie, included Peter, Paul and Mary, Stan Musial, John Wayne, Audie Murphy, and John Glenn. Well, Holy Idealist, what did these folks have in common? They stood for something good, they had character, they sought perfection and served as role models.

In the '50s and '60s, we still used an operator to place phone calls; computers, cell phones, cable TV, Walmart, and terrorists, all lay in the future. We now say that was a simpler time. Maybe it was, but we still stressed out over tests, girlfriends and boyfriends, the bomb, enough money to fill up the gas tank of our parents' car after a Saturday night cruising Main Street. As kids, we could fill a Saturday by ourselves playing with nothing but a stick and a rock. We didn't depend on soccer moms to ferry us to our overfilled schedule of organized activities. We explored, discovered, and made mistakes. We were trusted to spend all day doing whatever we did, coming home with few questions asked. All that developed character.

Each of us has a different memory, both good and bad. Collectively, those memories are what we pass on. They are what made us who we are. No matter what school we went to, what church we attended, what doctor we visited, we were the Tuscola we all remember. Each small town across America did something similar. As we sit by the fire now, hair gray or white, or none at all, grandchildren or great-grandchildren by our side, we can smile as we think of what the Strand was and what it meant. We can pass on the memories, but our feelings remain as part of us.

We can compare those times now, and it grows and looms in its distant magnificence. It might not have been that good after all, but it was ours. There were laughs and smiles, tears, and frowns. We learned what love was and what it wasn't. We failed and we succeeded. But we all had one thing that will only get better and better as we fade away. We were lost in the Sixties once and we found our way out. We focus on the good, the happiness, the friends, the joys of our own lifetimes.

In retrospect, it was a simpler time and we all know what I mean. I'm not sure I could explain it to a high school graduate today. The old saying still fits: you had to be there. Parking a car in Ervin Park on a Saturday afternoon in May, listening to that new group called the Beatles, wondering where Viet Nam was, hearing about the new actress Angie Dickenson, going up to Pesotum where Highway 45 crossed the new Interstate being constructed, and trying out that new invention called the skateboard. What we now refer to as the Sixties was still in the future, but was very soon to hit us between the eyes. It was the calm before the storm. We thought the times were good, and they were.

THIRTY

Last One Standing

In the year 2000, on one of my last visits to see my dad—when he was 95—my friend Mike Carroll gave me a tattered copy of *The Tuscolian, Class of 1925*. On the first page, I was shocked to see the book was dedicated to Miss Harriett J. Sluss. Her picture showed an attractive young woman who looked nothing like the elderly woman I had for freshman Latin in 1962. Also pictured was Dorothy Deer, a young woman who was just starting her teaching career. Miss Sluss and Miss Deer taught my father, mother, brother, and me over a period of decades.

I sat down with Dad to look through the book—1925 was his graduating class. He kept repeating these words as we looked at the class of 24 girls and 12 boys: "she is dead, he is dead…" When he finished, he said rather quietly, but with little emotion, "Looks like I'm the last one standing."

Seventy-five years after the pictures were taken of the 1925 Tuscola High School graduating class, all but he had left this earth. They attended the old high school, which we later called the new North Ward. I had walked the same halls and sat in the same classrooms as a 7th and 8th grader that he had as a senior in high school.

I was home to attend the 35th reunion of the class of 1965. I had been reliving in my mind my high school days, but this remembrance of the past with my father made me realize what had changed for him. All his classmates were dead. His world had changed beyond recognition, even though he lived in the same town he did 75 years ago.

I didn't give that much more thought as I attended the reunion and awakened old memories. But as I began putting this book together, after missing the 50th reunion in 2015, I thought once again about such a vision: the last one standing. One of our group of almost one hundred will be the last one standing. We don't have any idea who that will be. But it will come to someone in the hopefully distant future. At the 50th reunion, our class had lost about ten members. Now as we are past 70 years of age, we are facing this fact: we are starting to fade out. Who will have the distinction of being the very last one?

When we were together creating our senior yearbook in 1965, no one gave it a thought. We were young, energetic, full of dreams, ambitions, plans—just like the class of 1925. Most do not want to think thoughts like these, but life is gradually overcoming us. We are slowly leaving, and in the not too distant future, that process will speed up. We will thin out, carrying memories and dreams with us, leaving historians and great-grandchildren to keep the memories alive. Someday, someone will find a tattered copy of *The Tuscolian*, 1965, and go over it with an aged father or mother and ask who is still left. He or she will look at page after page, and say, "Looks like I'm the last one standing."

I don't mean this to be morbid, but we are facing a fact. Our memories of the good times, of the town we called hometown, our friends, playmates, and classmates, will be gone except within one person. He or she will represent the rest of us. And it doesn't matter whether Tuscola, Illinois, was your hometown—we all have somewhere we call our hometown. As we grow older, we will face the importance of our memories, and the last one standing who shared all the memories may or may not still live in that town we called home. Will they tell others about people named Gus or Miss Sluss and a school like the North Ward? Will it be important to them? A town makes, and is made up of, its children. What we called hometown was important to us, but when we are gone, what will then be important to our children and great-grandchildren? Does it matter?

My childhood friends were Tuscola. We grew up there, attended schools, either left or stayed, but we made Tuscola what it was for a time. We were part of a place and a time that is now gone. Until that one last time when there is no home left, except in our minds. Then you walk towards the sunset and leave the past to history. Then we will be gone, even the *last one standing*. As the winds blew off a distant glacier to the north, waving the prairie grass while the herds of bison grazed off into the distance, our memories will hover like an apparition, then disappear over the horizon.

The Legacy: Looking into the Sunrise

ALL OF US, whether we grew up in a town called Tuscola, in a time mid-twentieth century or later, share common memories. These memories are of experiences and adventures in a specific place and a general time. These memories become stories. The stories involve each of us and involve other people, other shared memories, and when combined with the story of the remaining years of adulthood, add up to something we call our lives. Our life, when carried forward and not backward in time, is what becomes our legacy. It is our life, our values, our achievements, our philosophy of life, our memories—all things which define someone unique in the history of the world. There has never been anyone with those experiences and stories. Nor will there ever be again. The places have changed; the time has changed. Parts of that story may resemble others, but it is ours alone. When we are gone, and we will all be someday, the legacy remains. What will it be?

I have shared stories of my hometown, my childhood, a few of my memories. However, it is not about me. It is a story I was part of and it forms a part of the entire story of my life. However, the remainder of my life was shaped and molded by my hometown and my childhood. I hope readers will think of how their memories defined the rest of their lives. The story each of us tells is about good times as well as not so good; it is about smiles and tears, successes and failures, adventures, and quiet times. A good story is something to keep adjusting as we may remember new things or forget others. Memories have a funny way of telling us what we think to be important. Sometimes, we may not realize something was valuable until we lose it to the fog of time. If we can revive memories forgotten, that is more valuable than any treasure.

If you have not yet done so, share your stories with children and grandchildren. They will be the ones to carry forward your legacy. You may reveal a part of you others didn't know. It may even help shape their lives.

ꜱ

I have written much about the past—my remembrances of a Tuscola over half a century ago. I have stood looking into the sunset, into a history that I know a lot about. I lived it and it is now gone. There is no mystery. In my other writings, I talk often about getting into a time machine—with all of my time machine travels in the deep past. It is much safer that way. I know how things end.

I now want to turn around and look into the sunrise. The sunrise is about looking into the future. A time yet to happen, where the outcome is unknown. There is a high level of discomfort in doing this. It is about uncertainty, maybe a little fear. It is history yet to occur.

I think of a place and time that I will never know. Nor will you. Look to a time a century from now. What will Tuscola be like? Will it still be here? It has certainly endured for over a century and a half. Much happened before the time in the Tuscola I knew and grew up with. The town led an active life before I was a part of it; it will certainly lead an active life after all of us here today are gone.

But what of the future, many years beyond what you or I will see? Will your great-grandchildren tell stories of their past, which happens to be our future yet unknown? Can we even understand such a future-past? Tuscola didn't exist five hundred years ago; will it exist five hundred years from now? Humans didn't walk this prairie forty thousand years ago; will they walk this land forty thousand years from now?

Whenever I've fantasized about traveling in time, it was always the past I wished to visit. I know the story. I know what happened in all those intervening years. I guess I want to see it as it was. I want to know what I missed. The future? It might scare me. It might tell me what I did or didn't do correctly. We all fear uncertainty. Looking far into the future might scare us all. And if we know what the future is or will be, would that affect what we do now? Can we change the future if we don't like what we see years from now?

These are all academic questions. And they are worth thinking about. Our actions today depend on what happened long ago. The past gave us what we have today. And our actions today will determine what happens long into the future. Our descendants in one hundred years will blame us or thank us for what we do today. It is not too late to change the future.

It is said in the Tsalagi (Cherokee) tradition that in the first six years of life the child is completely formed and will show you the person he or she will become. Many adults will still be motivated by those early patterns set down in childhood. It is a wise practitioner who carefully changes the thought form of habit and sets a path for certainty through understanding his or her own nature, pulling threads of early patterns and reweaving them into a beauteous garment.

Dhyani Ywahoo, *Voices of Our Ancestors*

ACKNOWLEDGMENTS

I have written parts of this over the past forty years, wavering back and forth, deciding to put my writing into a book, then backing out. I occasionally sent chapters to members of my Class of '65. Some of them commented. I thank them for their support. I especially thank two members who relentlessly encouraged me over the years: Donna Ard Braden and Anne Ferguson Monahan.

I thank Dave Porter, editor and publisher of the Tuscola Review for printing some of the chapters as part of an advertising insert in 2019. I also thank the advertisers of that insert who sponsored it. I published chapters on my Facebook page and was encouraged by other Tuscolians, some of whom I have never met.

One of my biggest supporters is my classmate Michael Gale Carroll. One of my oldest friends from childhood, Mike graciously sponsored more of my chapters in the *Tuscola Review* insert as part of his advertising for his housing development on the grounds of the old high school. Mike also wrote the Introduction, while at the time writing his own book. A big thanks to Jon Oye who furnished old photos from his Tuscola collection. Sharon Rose Capie supplied the old plat of Tuscola which serves as the book cover. Anna Miller, director of Douglas County Museum in Tuscola, searched archives for photos; unfortunately, old images of Gus's are not to be found—you will need to go to Tuscola and experience Gus's yourself. A big thanks also to those old friends who supplied reviews. They knew Tuscola as I did and appreciated the memories.

Any author will confirm that finding a good editor is one of the hardest things in publishing a book. I have tried several for past books, but none were as effective as Katherine. It may seem tricky having a spouse as an editor but she made the book come together. More than simple thanks for her work.

PHOTO CREDITS

JAC: Author's collection of Ruby Colwell photos
TJ: *Tuscola Journal*
JO: Jon Oye Collection
DCM: Douglas County Museum Collection
GN: Gary Neal
AFM: Anne Ferguson Monahan
TCHS: Tuscola High School Yearbooks
SRC: Sharon Rose Capie Collection
KLC: Katherine Colwell

Cover Tuscola map / SRC
78 Keyed Tuscola map detail / SRC
80 R.B. Colwell / JAC
80 Ruby Hance Colwell / JAC
81 Author with Wiggles on snow mountain / JAC
81 Main St view / JO
82 Library / JO
82 Post Office / JO
83 Post Office mural / JO
83 Courthouse / JO
84 Jarman Hospital / JO
84 Hotel Douglas / JO / GN
84 USI-Petro / JO
85 Old North Ward School / JO
86 Third Grade / JAC
86 New North Ward School / JO
87 South Ward School / JO
87 TCHS view / TCHS 1959 / JO
88 Leaf collection / JAC
88 Strand / DCM
89 Ervin Park / JO
89 Little League / JAC
90 Band uniform / JAC
90 C. Kohrt / JAC / TJ
91 Halloween / JAC
91 Nixon / JAC / TJ
92 Class of 1965 / TCHS 1965 / KLC
92 Class 50th reunion / AFM
179 About the author / KLC / JAC